# WRT 150

## A Guide to First-Year Writing at Grand Valley State University

11th Edition
2012-13

Edited by
Dauvan Mulally

Grand Valley State University
Allendale, Michigan

TAPESTRY PRESS, LTD.
Littleton, MA 01460

Printed in the United States of America

ISBN 978-1-59830-573-9

# Contents

# First-Year Writing at Grand Valley

## Introduction

Welcome to the Department of Writing's first-year writing program at Grand Valley State University. Our courses improve your writing, critical thinking, and information literacy skills. In this course, you will gain abilities that will carry over into the rest of your university experience, and beyond. The goal of this book, A Guide to First-Year Writing at Grand Valley State University, is just that—to guide you in your writing endeavors. From here on, we will just call this book the Guide. As a community of writers, we have worked to create a Guide that invites you into our community and celebrates student writing at all stages. We hope you will make extensive use of this Guide, both in class and on your own, to succeed in our required first-year writing course, Writing 150 ("WRT 150" in the Grand Valley catalog).

Our Department of Writing strives to create a consistent program for all students who take WRT 150. Our professors teach WRT 150 using their own preferred teaching methods, but important elements remain consistent across all sections. We have standardized foundational elements like course objectives, grading criteria, grading methods, and departmental policies—all of which you will find explained in this book. Each semester every WRT 150 teacher meets once a week with other teachers to discuss these course goals and expectations as they apply to particular students' papers. At the end of the term, these groups of teachers read final portfolios of the work that students produce in WRT 150 and assign each portfolio a grade. As a result, at Grand Valley, you can compare your grade at the end of your first-year writing experience fairly with the grade of every other student on campus who has taken WRT 150.

This Guide tells you more about our shared course expectations for WRT 150. At the beginning, we provide brief descriptions of the other courses that you might take before taking WRT 150, just in case you wish to reconsider your choice of the right place to start your college writing experience. Then we provide a much more detailed guide to WRT 150. First, we provide course policies. Next, to help you understand how to prepare your work for portfolio grading, we include our WRT 150 portfolio submission guidelines. Then we provide descriptions of our grading standards—the same descriptions that we use when we grade your portfolios. After the grading descriptions, we offer further information about keys to success in WRT 150. We also provide information about support that we offer to help you succeed.

After that discussion, we include several A level portfolios from last year's WRT 150 students to guide your revisions and spur classroom discussion of the grading expectations. Finally, we also include effective student writing from a range of academic courses around campus.

## Other Course Options

As you know by now, you decide which writing course you should take first at Grand Valley, after considering information about our departmental requirements and consulting with advisors during orientation. You have these three choices:

- ESL 098 is for second-language students making a transition to standard written English.
- WRT 098 is for students who need more practice and instruction to develop fluency and fullness in their writing.
- WRT 150 is for students who write fluently and are ready to begin college-level academic writing, including writing with sources.

About 85 percent of students who enter Grand Valley place themselves into WRT 150—a four-credit course designed to prepare you for writing in your college classes. If you are reading this Guide, you have already made that choice. Just in case you would like to consider your choice one more time, here are brief descriptions of your other options. If you have doubts about the course you have chosen, talk about your concerns with your professor as soon as possible. Your professor may also assign a quick writing task during the first week of the course, in part to help you make that decision.

## ESL 098

Specialists in second language learning teach ESL 098, offered by the Department of English. It is the best starting place for students for whom English language provides more difficulty than writing itself. In particular, students who are highly successful writers in another language but who have difficulty writing in English should take ESL 098 rather than WRT 098.

## WRT 098

WRT 098 focuses on raising students' confidence in their writing, assisting them in gaining agency and control over their writing and education, and encouraging them to value a lifelong engagement with writing and reading. Students write to learn as well as to communicate, and they learn more about the practice of writing, particularly writing in college. The course invites spontaneity and discovery, seeking to develop in students the kinds of habits and writing strategies that will enable them to succeed in WRT 150 and beyond.

WRT 098 emphasizes immersion, invention, and revision. Students write continually, generating new drafts all semester long. Students learn invention strategies to get papers started, learn to keep the writing process going to produce a substantial volume of writing, and develop positive attitudes toward writing. Revision, by which we mean truly re-seeing and re-imagining each new draft, helps students develop the habits by which highly effective writers continue to improve the quality of their writing before turning to final editing. WRT 098 features peer workshop groups led by trained writing consultants from The Fred Meijer Center for Writing (the "Writing Center"), so that students learn not only the benefits of seeking assistance from the Writing Center but also the value of thoughtful peer review.

Students in WRT 098 receive a preliminary introduction to college-level research skills, using the Internet and the more advanced research materials available through Grand Valley's library and the library's online resources. WRT 098 also introduces students to using computers in ways that WRT 150 will require. Students who need more help with these more technical aspects of college writing may also want to start in WRT 098.

## Overview of WRT 150

As the single writing course required of all Grand Valley students, WRT 150 focuses on academic writing, including writing informed by scholarly research. Teachers assume that you are ready to read, summarize, and analyze a wide variety of college-level published material. They also assume that you have experience with narrative, descriptive, and argumentative writing. In most WRT 150 classes, you first write four or five papers, at least one of which integrates material from highly credible sources that you find in the course of doing significant academic research. In most cases, these papers will be four to ten pages long in normal academic format. From among these papers, you will pick three, including at least one that demonstrates your research skills and strategies, to include in your final portfolio for grading. Then, you will spend a considerable amount of time revising and improving your three portfolio papers.

In WRT 150, you encounter challenging reading material—whether you find it in assigned readings or in your own research materials—and you practice discussing, summarizing, and analyzing that material. You also work on developing writing processes that can help you complete new kinds of writing tasks and rise to new levels of writing ability—processes that move effectively from prewriting, inventing, planning, and drafting to revising, consulting, editing, and finishing.

In most sections, half of your WRT 150 class meetings take place in a computer classroom. Each computer is connected to the Internet and the Grand Valley network. The Grand Valley network includes personal storage space on the campus server and special access to research sources maintained by Grand Valley's library system. WRT 150 teachers assume that you have a basic familiarity with computers, word processors, web browsers, and email.

By the end of WRT 150, as an experienced college writer you should be able to:

## Prewrite, Invent, and Plan

- Read and understand material written for college audiences.
- Develop clearly focused written summaries, analyses, and paraphrases that demonstrate an understanding of the material you have read.
- Develop ideas using a variety of prewriting techniques, which may include brainstorming, freewriting, journal-keeping, consulting with others, conducting library research, and analyzing your audiences.

## Revise, Develop, and Shape

- Develop writing from early, writer-oriented drafts to later, reader-oriented drafts.
- Produce effective writing for a variety of purposes, such as narrating, explaining, exploring, and persuading.
- Demonstrate the ability to focus your writing on supportable themes, claims, or theories.
- Support your focus using well-selected details that are suggestive, accurate, and relevant.
- Consult with peer reviewers and other readers to assess the further needs of your drafts.
- Revise writing with particular audiences in mind, including academic audiences.
- Conduct effective, significant scholarly research.
- Integrate facts and opinions from a variety of sources into your own writing.

## Refine, Edit, and Finish

- Include words, facts, and ideas from research sources in ways that fully credit the original source and avoid plagiarism.
- Control the main features of a specific documentation style (like MLA or APA).
- Refine your sentence structures to produce an effective style and voice.
- Edit writing so that academic audiences can read the writing without having their attention and understanding diverted by problems in grammar, spelling, punctuation, and format.

In addition to requiring WRT 150, Grand Valley supports the development of your writing ability in other courses. Many General Education courses focus on developing your writing in specific academic areas. You do not need to finish WRT 150 before taking those classes. They work along with WRT 150 to develop your writing foundation. After building that foundation, you will take two courses in disciplines of interest to you specifically designated as Supplemental Writing Skills courses. You may also take further writing courses, and many of your college courses will involve extensive writing. Thus, WRT 150 is not the end of your college writing instruction. Instead, it seeks to supply you with an important foundation for further development.

# University and Writing Department Policies

## WRT 150 Course Policies

WRT 150 sections can have many differences in terms of assignments, daily routines, and instruction. We want all teachers to teach in the ways that best suit their abilities and the needs of their particular students. Nevertheless, as part of our effort to ensure consistency across sections, all WRT 150 teachers adhere to the following university and departmental policies.

## Required Passing Grade

You must pass WRT 150 with a grade of C or better (above C-) to satisfy Grand Valley's Writing Skills Requirement. If you do not receive a grade of C or better, you will need to take WRT 150 again.

## Learning or Physical Disabilities

If you have any special needs because of learning, physical, or any other disabilities, please contact Disability Support Services at 616-331-2490. Any student needing academic accommodations beyond those given to the entire class needs to request assistance from DSS. Writing faculty work with DSS to accommodate students' special needs and devise a plan that is fair to all students. Furthermore, if you have a disability and think you will need assistance evacuating a classroom and/or building in an emergency situation, please make your teacher and DSS aware so that Grand Valley can develop a plan to assist you.

## Attendance

Regular, timely, and full attendance is required to succeed in WRT 150. According to the Grand Valley catalog, teachers may fail students for excessive absences. In WRT 150, missing class more than four times constitutes excessive absences, and can be grounds for failing the course. Tardiness, leaving class while it is in session, and coming unprepared may also count as an absence or partial absence according to your teacher's policies. Your teacher should send you an email warning after the fourth absence. If you miss class or come unprepared after such a warning, you will be ineligible to submit a final portfolio for the course, which means you will fail. Excessive absence itself is the grounds for failure, so that lack of warning does not excuse your absences. The warning simply provides additional clarity.

## WRT 150 Goals

By the end of WRT 150, your final portfolio should demonstrate that you have achieved the program's goals and can perform each of these tasks:

### Content and Development:
- Offer readers a clear purpose for reading.
- Maintain a single focus throughout the entire paper.
- Present ideas and descriptions that engage a college-level audience in your discussion.
- Conduct college-level research to find credible source material for a variety of purposes.
- Present a claim or focus that is developed with discussion, details, and examples, including graphics when useful.
- Discover and integrate sufficient material from outside sources to demonstrate your abilities in college level writing, research, and thinking.

### Organization:
- Establish an overall pattern for a paper to follow.
- Progress from one point, idea, or scene to another in a coherent, logical way.
- Construct paragraphs that are generally well-organized within the overall pattern of a paper.
- Lead readers through the order of your discussion in obvious and helpful ways.

### Style:
- Craft sentences with purposefully chosen words and phrases.
- Structure sentences effectively to be clear, logical, and readable
- Use a variety of sentence structures for good reasons.
- Maintain an overall voice in each paper that is appropriate for its purpose, genre, and audiences.

**Mechanics:**

- Adopt a format that is acceptable and appropriate for academic writing.
- Refer to outside sources that are introduced, integrated, and documented.
- Attend carefully to grammar, spelling, punctuation, and usage in final, edited writing.
- Use with care a standard academic style guide, such as the MLA or APA style guides.

# WRT 150 Portfolio Guidelines

## Portfolio Grading

We determine all final grades in WRT 150 by evaluating a final portfolio containing three of your papers. Your own teacher's portfolio grading group grades your portfolio. We use this method so that our grading can be as fair and accurate as possible. Our teachers work very hard to make sure that this method gives you the fairest result.

Your teacher's portfolio grading group (usually four to six teachers) reads and discusses samples of writing from their classes throughout the semester to agree about standards for A, B, C, and D papers. Their standards begin with those established by the Writing Department and set forth more specifically further on in this Guide, at pages 15-23. Through their discussions, the groups work to fit those standards more specifically to your assignments and the work done by your class.

At the end of the semester, your teacher and one other teacher from the portfolio grading group will read and grade your portfolio. If they disagree about the grade, a third teacher in that group reads your portfolio and decides which reader, your teacher or the other teacher, has come closest to the standards that the portfolio group has agreed upon during the semester. Agreement between two or more teachers determines your letter grade in the class. For example, if your portfolio receives a B from the first two readers, you receive a B on your portfolio. If your portfolio receives an A from one reader, a B from another, and an A from a third reader, you receive an A on your portfolio. By using this method, we seek to arrive at a "community" grade based on the quality of your writing rather than a grade based solely on one teacher's preferences or on your teacher's personal opinion of you.

Once the portfolio grading group arrives at a letter grade, your teacher also has the option of adding a "plus" or "minus" to the final letter grade based on other aspects of your work, such as attendance, class participation, effective peer-review, and completion of reading assignments. Teachers should not raise or lower your grade any further than a plus or minus, which ensures the highest degree of fairness based on the quality of your work.

The portfolios are graded after class is over, and students should keep their own copies of papers, so the portfolios are not returned. For those reasons, we do not write comments on the papers or the portfolios. Teachers do often write very brief notes about grades of D so that students receiving this grade may ask about the reasons for that grade.

If you have any questions about the grade that you receive, ask your teacher to discuss your grade with you.

## Semester-long Evaluation

The fact that you earn your grade with your final portfolio does not mean that the evaluation of your writing should be a mystery. First, you should learn how to apply the grading criteria to your own writing. Your teacher should read your writing throughout the semester and respond to it with comments and suggestions for revision. Many teachers will have you read, comment on, and evaluate other students' work. For most students, a grade is not necessary for early drafts because the proper focus is on what the paper could become, not on what it is. But if you want a grade on an assignment and your teacher has not given one, just ask. Teachers will be able to tell you where they think the paper falls within the range of A to D. Your teacher will probably tell you what the portfolio group has been saying about writing like yours.

Nevertheless, it is important to remember that all grade estimates—whether they are by you, your teacher, your classmates, or your Aunt Lou—are just that: estimates. Ultimately, the grade will depend on the entire portfolio in its final form, something nobody will be able to review carefully until the end of the term. Mainly what you need to do is just keep on working. If the teacher says your paper is probably a low B or a C, your next question should be: "What could I work on in this paper that would improve it?" Improve your research and your writing until the very last day, and you will receive the best grade available to you. Meanwhile, you should also seek to improve your own judgment of your own grade, using the grading criteria. The most successful and satisfied WRT 150 students do not need the teacher to tell them what grade they are getting; they already have a fairly good idea themselves.

## Midterm Evaluation

Grand Valley requires midterm grade reports for first-year students and some upper-level students. Midterm grades are available on the web but not recorded on your official transcript. Midterm grades in WRT 150 can only assess the overall quality of your work in the class up to that point and your prospects for doing better. Such assessments have no direct bearing on your final grade because we base WRT 150 grades on the quality of your writing at the end of the term, as determined by portfolio grading. For a full explanation of your midterm grade, please consult with your teacher.

## Your Final Portfolio

### Evaluation Procedures

Many professionals use portfolios to show other people what they are capable of producing. Your WRT 150 portfolio represents your own end-of-semester writing capabilities. The portfolio includes three fully revised and polished papers, including at least one that integrates outside sources and accurately credits the ideas and language drawn from those sources. Together, these three pieces of writing produce the bulk of your final course grade.

The three papers in your portfolio represent your abilities as a college-level academic writer, so you should select them with care. For example, you probably do not want three very short papers, since that would fail to show your ability to write a longer paper. Ask your teacher and peer review-ers about your selections if you are not sure. Your teacher and the other students should help you make good choices about what goes in the final portfolio. Also, read the full portfolios published in this book, and, to-gether with your teacher and classmates, try to generalize from them what constitutes a strong WRT 150 portfolio.

As explained earlier in this Guide, your WRT 150 portfolio is read and evaluated by at least two members of a group of teachers, including your own professor, that meets regularly throughout the term to discuss grading criteria and expectations. Your readers supply one grade per portfolio; that is, they do not grade the individual papers, but rather the entire portfolio. Your first priority should be to include your best writing, but your second priority should be to demonstrate your ability to perform a range of academic writing tasks. Of course, as part of that range of academic writing tasks, you must demonstrate that you can conduct responsible academic research and integrate a variety of reputable sources into your writing.

**So that your teacher has time to check all work for any problems, we strictly enforce your teachers' requirements for turning in earlier versions of work that you intend to place in your portfolio.** All papers in your portfolio must have been assigned for the class and seen by your teacher in draft form before final submission.

### Submission Guidelines

Your final portfolio will consist of three final papers, each individually stapled. Papers should be printed on a letter-quality printer. If your teacher gives no special instructions, follow these further guidelines. Margins should be one inch all the way around the page and lines should be double-spaced. Fonts should be common or default types (Arial, Calibri, Times New Roman, etc.), and the point-size should be close to standard typeface (11 or 12 points). If your teacher has special instructions for the form or format of your papers, the portfolio grading groups will honor those instructions.

In addition to requiring you to submit earlier drafts, your teacher is entitled to set further requirements before your portfolio will be eligible for grading. Common requirements are that you attend class regularly, submit papers on time in response to individual assignments, use particular formats, or submit papers at a specific length or level of editing care. If you do not meet your teacher's specific requirements, your teacher may refuse to submit your portfolio for grading, in which case you will fail the course. Such requirements should be set out clearly in your teacher's syllabus, assignments, or other written instructions.

Submit your papers in a standard manila file folder with your first initial, last name, and section clearly written on the filing tab. Your portfolio is due to your teacher by the end of the last class before finals week, unless your teacher's syllabus sets a different deadline. If your portfolio is late, you may fail the course.

The portfolio grading groups do not comment on portfolios except for brief notes on D portfolios, so portfolios are not returned. You should keep copies of your work and wait for grade reports to see your course grades. If there are questions about your grade, you should speak with your teacher. The Department may keep your portfolio and use it for internal studies of our teaching and its results, but we will not publish the contents of your writing without your permission. Most teachers recycle the paper versions of your documents after the end of the semester following the one when you turned in the portfolio.

### Evaluation Criteria—Characteristics of A, B, C, and D Papers

We provide the general characteristics of A, B, and C portfolios for you here so that you can identify precisely how your work is evaluated. Characteristics that cause portfolios to fall below the standard for a passing grade are presented as characteristics of D papers. Factors that can cause you to receive an F for the course are listed at the end of the grading criteria. Your teacher, with the help of the teacher's portfolio grading group, will develop more specific understandings of these criteria to apply to your exact assignments and portfolios; in doing so, however, all of them will be seeking to apply the general characteristics below accurately and fairly to your work.

Our approach does mean that we do not reward effort unless it produces results. We want to ensure that what counts as A, B, C, D, or F will be roughly the same for every student in every section, based on achievement.

# Characteristics of A Papers

Content and Research

- The portfolio consistently engages the interest of intelligent and sophisticated college-level readers.
- Papers effectively address and engage their likely and intended audiences.
- Papers succeed at accomplishing challenging purposes.
- Each paper maintains a consistent focus on the main claim or goal for the paper.
- Each paper develops its focus with significant and interesting discussion, details, and examples, including graphics when useful.
- The portfolio clearly demonstrates the writer's information literacy and ability to use college-level academic research as a significant means to develop the writer's ideas.
- The portfolio clearly demonstrates the writer's ability to introduce and integrate material from relevant outside sources in ways that advance the purposes for the writing and meet the expectations of intelligent and sophisticated college-level readers.

Organization

- Titles and opening sections of papers inform readers appropriately of the topic, purpose, and focus of the paper in ways that motivate readers to look forward to reading further.
- Paragraphs are purposefully organized and substantially developed with supporting evidence, examples, and reasoning.
- Paragraphs break information into parts that contribute to a greater understanding of the whole.
- Readers can easily see how the order in which information appears supports the focus and purpose of the papers.
- The papers lead readers through the order of the discussion in ways that are explicit, clear, and purposeful, including effective transition devices when needed.
- Readers can see a meaningful pattern in the order of the information as a whole.
- Closing sections give readers a satisfied sense that the purpose of the writing has been achieved.

Style

- Word choice is precise, interesting, and appropriate to the writing task and audience.
- Language is mature and purposefully controlled.
- Sentences are clear, logical, enjoyable, and easily understood by college-level readers.
- Sentences often make active statements and use efficient and effective modification.
- Sentence structure varies according to the content, purpose, and audience.
- A consistent voice complements each papers' purposes, fits its genres, and appeals to its likely and intended readers.
- Information and quotations from sources are integrated skillfully into the writer's own sentences and paragraphs.

Mechanics

- Format is consistent with the detailed requirements of an applicable style guide, such as the MLA or APA style guides.
- References to outside sources are cited and documented according to the appropriate style guide carefully enough that readers can easily identify the sources that have been quoted or referenced.
- Problems in grammar, spelling, punctuation, or usage do not interfere with communication.
- Editing shows respectful and effective attention to the desire of readers to read without being interrupted by unexpected errors or problems with documentation and format.

# Characteristics of B Papers

Content and Research

- The portfolio connects with the interest of intelligent and sophisticated college-level readers.
- Papers clearly address the expectations of their likely and intended audiences.
- Papers accomplish interesting purposes or make strong attempts to accomplish challenging purposes.
- Each paper maintains a consistent, single focus.
- Each paper develops a focus with fitting and relevant discussions, details, and examples, including graphics when useful.
- The portfolio demonstrates the writer's ability to use college-level academic research clearly and purposefully to develop the writer's ideas and improve the papers in which research is used.
- The portfolio demonstrates the writer's ability to introduce and integrate material from relevant outside sources in ways that enhance the accomplishment of goals and purposes.

Organization

- Titles and opening sections of papers are well-chosen and appropriate to the topic and focus of the papers.
- Paragraphs are clearly organized and adequately developed with supporting evidence, examples, and reasoning, though some paragraphs may lack richness of detail or evidence.
- Paragraphs break information into parts that make sense and assist effective reading.
- Readers can identify the focus of each paper and follow it through the entire discussion.
- Readers can identify how the order in which information appears supports the focus and purpose of the papers.
- Overall patterns in the order of presentation make sense.
- Transitions between and within paragraphs advance the writer's ideas.
- Closing sections give readers a clear sense that the writer is ending the discussion at a good place.

Style

- Word choice is generally appropriate to the writing task and audience.
- Language is generally mature and purposefully controlled.
- Sentences are generally clear, logical, and readable.
- Sentences typically make active statements, extended by efficient and effective modification.
- Sentences vary in structure and only occasionally are choppy, rambling, or repetitive.
- The voice in each paper is consistent and appropriate for the writer's purpose and the audience.
- Information and quotations from sources make sense within the writer's own sentences and paragraphs.

Mechanics

- Format is appropriate and generally follows the requirements of an assigned style guide, such as the MLA or APA style guides.
- References to outside sources are cited and documented according to the appropriate style guide carefully enough that readers can determine when source material has been used and find the sources.
- Problems in grammar, spelling, punctuation, or usage rarely interfere with communication.
- Editing shows diligent and informed attention to the desire of readers to read without being interrupted by unexpected errors.

# Characteristics of C Papers

Content and Research

- The portfolio makes sense to intelligent and sophisticated college-level readers, though it may not consistently hold their interest.
- The portfolio presents ideas and descriptions with readers in mind.
- Papers appear to aim at accomplishing purposes.
- Each paper generally maintains a single focus, though the focus may be on a topic or an event rather than an idea, claim or goal.
- Each paper generally develops a focus with details, examples, and discussions, including graphics when useful.
- The portfolio demonstrates the writer's ability to use relevant college-level academic research as a means to develop a topic.
- The portfolio demonstrates the writer's ability to include material from outside sources within the general requirements of an applicable style guide.

Organization

- Titles and openings generally match the topic and focus.
- Paragraphs make sense and usually use some evidence or detailed examples to support points.
- Papers generally establish an overall organizational pattern for readers to follow.
- Each paper develops a basic focus, with few paragraphs appearing to be out of sequence or off-track.
- Transitions from one section and idea to another are evident and make sense.

Style

- Most words appear to be well chosen and fit the purpose and audience for the particular paper.
- Most of the time sentences are not short and choppy, long and rambling, or vague and wordy.
- Sentences are generally readable and make sense.
- Sentences sometimes feature the efficient and effective uses of modifying clauses and phrases.

- The writer's voice is consistent and appropriate, usually fitting the writer's purpose, genre, and audience.
- Information and quoted language from sources is clearly presented as source material.

Mechanics

- Format choices are generally appropriate for the purposes of the papers.
- References to outside sources are generally cited and documented, if not always in the appropriate style; readers can determine when source material has been quoted or referenced, and instances of unreferenced source material are few, unimportant, and clearly not intentional.
- Mistakes in grammar, spelling, punctuation, or usage do not generally interfere with either the writer's credibility or the reader's ability to read the text easily.
- Editing shows adequate attention to the desire of readers to read without being interrupted by unexpected errors.

# D Portfolios

Regardless of writing ability, portfolios will receive the grade of D if, as a whole, the portfolio fails to demonstrate that the student understands how to conduct college-level research as well as how to integrate the results of such research into purposeful writing without committing plagiarism. Otherwise, D portfolios rarely have similar characteristics. The lists below present the danger signals that help predict when a portfolio does not demonstrate competence. The main key to avoiding a D is to meet the criteria for at least a C.

Content & Research

- Topics, purposes, claims, or focuses are so simplistic and obvious that they do not engage the interest of college-educated readers.
- Papers have no apparent and appropriate audiences.
- Papers have no clear purposes.
- At least one paper is clearly fictional.
- Papers lack a single focus.
- Ideas are stated, but they are not developed with details, examples, and discussions.
- Language or material from sources are consistently presented in ways that are very hard to follow.
- Unintentional, careless misuse of source material would amount to plagiarism had it been intentional.
- The portfolio shows weak research and information literacy abilities, such as the use of very few sources, little variety of sources, or little obvious effort to conduct scholarly or professional research.
- Sources do not support and may even contradict the views that the writer attributes to them.

Organization

- Openings and endings are missing, misleading, or overly general.
- Readers cannot readily see the focus of the papers.
- Paragraphs frequently seem unrelated to each other or repetitive.
- Paragraphs do not develop logically from start to finish, or they break in illogical places.
- Paragraphs often end without developing broad, general statements

with evidence and reasoning.

- Transitions between and within paragraphs are weak, ineffective, or misleading.
- The papers do not establish clear patterns for readers to follow.

Style

- Sentences often are short and choppy, long and rambling, or vague and wordy.
- Disordered sentence parts, poor phrasing, and poor word choices make reading difficult.
- Sentences often disregard the normal rules of standard written English in ways that make ideas hard to understand.
- The voice often appears inappropriate for the writer's purpose, genre, and audience.

Mechanics

- Format, including any use of graphics, is extremely careless or entirely disregards the basic requirements of applicable style guides.
- Language or material from outside sources is not clearly cited.
- Documentation style is generally wrong according to the assigned style guide, often in ways that interfere with readers' abilities to find the source material and locate the referenced portions of the sources.
- Instances of misused source material show careless inattention to important requirements for quoting, paraphrasing, and citing, raising questions of possible plagiarism.
- Many errors in spelling, grammar, punctuation, word choice, and usage make reading difficult, or they strongly limit the writer's credibility.

# F Grades

The grade of F in WRT 150 is reserved for the following circumstances:

- The student did not turn in a portfolio by the last day of class (or the due date set by the teacher's syllabus, if the teacher chooses another due date).
- The portfolio did not have three papers in it that qualified for the portfolio under this Guide and the teacher's syllabus.
- The student violated course polices set by this Guide or the teacher's syllabus (for example, an attendance policy), if the information made clear that the violation would result in a grade of F.
- The student violated other policies of Grand Valley State University that clearly state that the violation could result in a grade of F.
- The student clearly committed plagiarism, as described by Grand Valley's Student Code, this Guide, and the teacher's syllabus.
- The portfolio clearly demonstrates a complete indifference to earning any higher grade.

**Grade Appeals**

If for any reason you need to appeal your final grade, please consult the Student Code for the applicable procedures. Your first contact should be with the teacher of your class. Appeals from your teacher's decision to the Department of Writing should be directed to Keith Rhodes, the Director of WRT 150, and be supported by a written appeal explaining how your portfolio displays the characteristics of the grade that you are seeking. Appeals to the Director of WRT 150 may be forwarded by e-mail at rhode-kei@gvsu.edu or delivered to the Department of Writing directed to the attention of the Director of WRT 150.

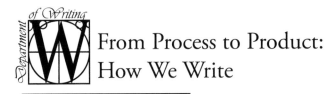

# From Process to Product: How We Write

## Writing as a Process

When we think of writers, we might imagine people who possess some magical talent that allows them to sit down and instantly put their thoughts into writing. But after observing experienced writers working from start to finish through real writing projects, researchers have concluded that expert writers do not simply sit down and "put it in writing" in one magical step. Rather, expert writers work through a complex series of steps, or "process." Different writers follow different steps depending on their needs and personal preferences, but in general expert writers experience writing as a process that unfolds over time, not as a "one and done" burst of inspiration.

For instance, when faced with the need to communicate to an audience, expert writers begin by exploring their own knowledge, feelings, and beliefs and often consult the knowledge, feelings, and beliefs of others, searching for something specific to say. Then they explore their communication options—the various forms available to them—before sketching out, reconsidering, revising, and polishing their message, making sure they are sensitive to their readers. Often, at several points during the writing process, expert writers ask friends or peers—people no more expert than they are, and often less so—to take a look at their drafted material and give advice or feedback. Finally, when satisfied with their efforts, expert writers polish the results and deliver their writing to their intended audience.

The example above illustrates five basic parts of a successful writing process:

- Prewriting and Inventing: generating ideas; forming questions for investigation and constructing a research plan; collecting, evaluating, and managing information; identifying possible subjects, purposes, audiences, and forms;
- Planning and Drafting: trying out ideas and approaches; zeroing in

on a single focus and a single form;

- Consulting: talking with people about preliminary ideas, plans, and drafts; soliciting oral and written feedback from friends and colleagues concerning content, structure, audience appeal, style, and correctness;
- Revising and Shaping: considering additions and deletions; reshaping and refocusing existing material, and editing for style, flow, and obvious error;
- Editing and Finishing: taking authorial responsibility for the final product; editing carefully for correctness and format; and delivering the final product to its intended audience (teacher, relative, client, committee, editor, etc.).

While you will probably have a unique way of going through the steps set out above, at some point all expert writers need to find ways of addressing the concerns of each step effectively. As teachers of WRT 150, we are not merely judges of your writing. In fact, you might best view teachers as coaches whose primary goal is to help you develop processes that you will use for the writing you do in WRT 150, in future Grand Valley classes, and on the job. We help you explore your writing processes through class information, class discussions, stimulating writing assignments, and responses to your writing in progress.

Your teacher will help you explore your writing processes, but you can take control of your own processes by considering the following checklist that we have devised to help you develop expert methods.

**Prewriting and Inventing:**

- Use a variety of brainstorming techniques to generate, develop, and focus topics.
- Write informally in journals or notebooks as an ongoing writer's activity.
- Use writing as a tool for learning as well as communicating.
- Analyze audience as a method of planning and focusing.
- Consider purpose, style, and form in relation to audience during the planning stages.
- Weigh a variety of form and style options during the planning stages.

- Sequence and initiate your own writing process to suit immediate purposes.
- Generate and select your own methods for developing material.
- Engage in prewriting discussions with your instructor and peers.
- Read as a writer; read published materials critically.
- Write and speak about yourself as a writer.
- Form questions for investigation and construct a research plan.
- Collect, evaluate, and manage information.
- Use basic reference materials (dictionary, encyclopedia, online search engine).
- Use research as a form of generating ideas and planning writing.
- Consider how numerical and graphic information might support your focus and purpose.

**Planning and Drafting:**
- Translate prewriting activities into drafts.
- Adapt your writing for specific readers, including academic ones.
- Write for broad, public, academic audiences.
- Vary diction and tone according to audience.
- Establish and maintain a focus that has a purpose.
- Maintain a consistent style throughout the different parts.
- Cultivate an appropriate and interesting voice.
- Integrate ideas and information from outside sources.
- Support ideas and observations with details, including numerical and graphic information.
- Use a word processor to capture your writing and save different versions when you make important changes.

**Consulting:**
- Use feedback from peers.
- Give feedback to peers.
- Engage in revision discussions with your instructor, peers, and writing consultant.
- Survey and integrate readers' needs and interests.
- Write alternate and more fully realized new versions of earlier drafts.
- Work productively in writing groups.

**Revising and Shaping:**

- Write and use your own evaluations of your drafts.
- Adapt the style and voice of your language to suit your purpose and audience.
- Revise for focus, development, order, structure, balance, and emphasis.
- Align the information and reasoning in the paper with the paper's focus.
- Add, delete, change, or recast material to suit your purposes and readers.
- Establish a clear focus throughout the paper.
- Consider the full variety of readers for whom you might actually be writing.
- Revise paragraphing and sentences for greater clarity and interest.
- Achieve "closure" in later drafts; make sure the product can become a consistent whole work.

**Editing and Finishing:**

- Proofread all writing intended for public audiences.
- Use your word processor's editing software to help you spot possible areas for improvement.
- Refresh your editing eye and ear by using methods like reading aloud, reading sentences in reverse order, reading as if you were somebody else (like your favorite Uncle or Aunt), or putting the latest draft away for a day or two.
- Use a dictionary and handbook for editing.
- Check your documentation with a guide for your documentation style.
- Check your use of material from sources to be sure you are using source material ethically.

**Responding to Peer Writing**

While reviewing the written "Process-Skills Checklist" can be instrumental in improving your papers, you will find that spoken feedback can be particularly helpful as well in the drafting process. Therefore, you will play a vital role in this information exchange. By offering valuable feedback on other students' papers, you will increase your ability to think critically about your own writing and at the same time receive valuable feedback to help you improve your paper drafts. As you consider this part of the process, you should avoid closing the door with final negative or positive evaluations on students' papers. If you judge early drafts by saying "your opening is perfect" or "this is already an A paper," you encourage your peers to stop rethinking and rewriting their papers.

Your teacher will probably have many suggestions about how to do successful peer review. Probably the least valuable thing peers can do for each other, at least without specific teacher guidance, is trying to fix each other's sentence errors. Try to ignore even the errors that you see—at least at first—so that you can give readers feedback on their content, organization, and style. After all, those things will probably determine much more of their grade. You may not be an expert on grammar, but you are an expert on what the writing communicated to you. Give the writer the benefit of what you know best.

**Information Literacy**

As academic writers, we work in a world of information and opinion, so it is very common for us to refer to facts and ideas originally published in other sources, and then to quote and cite those sources in ways that carefully show where we got our information. Educators commonly refer to this ability as "information literacy." We focus on information literacy for three main reasons. First, we want readers to take us seriously because we have done our homework; we have taken the time to find out what the best experts on the subject have already said. Second, we want to give proper credit to those who have already written on the subject; after all, we want credit for our own work, so we afford others the same courtesy. Third, we want our readers to know that credible experts agree with us.

Doing that work well starts with doing excellent research—going beyond the world of mere opinions so easily available on the Internet and learning how to find, read, and use the kind of information on which true experts rely. Grand Valley's expert research librarians have developed "Information Literacy Core Competencies" (ILCCs) for college students, defining six main goals for college-level research.

According to the ILCCs, as a college-level researcher, you should learn to

- construct a question or problem statement,
- locate and gather information,
- evaluate sources,
- manage information,
- use information ethically, and
- communicate knowledge.

You will want to develop these abilities throughout your college career, but WRT 150 should give a strong basis in all these areas. In WRT 150 you will learn to construct research questions by developing a preliminary focus to help you manage the range of material that you might pursue. You will learn to create a plan for your search and identify the resources that will be available to help you (such as library guides, access to scholarly journals through online reference tools called "databases," and the research librarians themselves). You will learn to evaluate sources so that you use the most appropriate and effective materials rather than just the materials that pop up first in a web search. You will learn to manage information in ways that help you keep track of what you have found and lower the stress and anxiety of conducting complicated research. Of course, as we re-emphasize in many ways in this Guide, you will learn to use information ethically by giving other writers credit for what you have learned from them and for what they have written. By learning to cite sources correctly, you learn to avoid plagiarism, honor copyright, and participate expertly in academic discussions. Finally, we want you to communicate knowledge effectively by coming to understand the ways in which those academic discussions take place, and then by beginning to take your own place in those discussions.

We cannot overemphasize the importance of these information literacy competencies as part of an effective academic writing process. Information literacy does not always show up directly in grading criteria because it is essentially a process, not a product; yet information literacy will have a profound effect on the quality of your writing, and thus on your WRT 150 grades.

Furthermore, the benefits of information literacy go well beyond WRT 150. When you learn to include results from research into your writing effectively, you prepare yourself for success in later college work. Summarizing, paraphrasing, and quoting your sources effectively shows that you truly understand them. Citing and documenting your sources correctly proves not only that you understand your sources but also that you understand how academic writing works. Perhaps most importantly for first-year writers, working with sources in the right ways helps you to avoid charges of plagiarism. When we work with research sources, we have to take unusual care to make sure that readers know exactly what we are claiming as our own thinking and writing and exactly what came from someone else. We will resist discussing research, documentation, and plagiarism at great length here because all of that needs to be addressed far more extensively in your WRT 150 class. You must, however, be alert to the importance of using research material ethically in your WRT 150 experience.

**Documenting Sources**

We have referred above to "documentation" of sources, which may be a new term for you. Basically, "documentation" means giving readers a very precise way to know exactly where you got your language and information and when exactly you are using language or information from your sources. For example, you might have seen books that had "footnotes" at the bottom of the page, linked to small numbers inserted into the discussion. Those footnotes "document" the source of the information.

To make that reference work easier to do (in the long run!), academic writers have created several carefully defined "documentation styles," depending on the field or discipline in which they are writing. Most writers in the humanities use the documentation system of the Modern Language Association (MLA style), and this is the documentation style used most often in WRT 150 classes. Writers in the social sciences usually use the documentation system of the American Psychological Association (APA style), so some WRT 150 classes use, or at least permit, APA style. Both of these styles insert a brief reference to a source inside parentheses (often starting with an author's last name), and then add a list of sources at the end that you can find quickly by using the information in the parentheses. Most of the sample essays toward the end of this book use those documentation styles. If you have not worked with documentation very much, be sure to look at those examples so that you have a better idea of how they work.

You are likely to learn several documentation styles during your college career. We understand that this variety of documentation styles means that, for college students, documentation styles do not seem "easier" to use. Instead, they can seem confusing, trivial, picky, and even cruel. Please try to keep an open mind about them. By the time you are done with college, you will settle into some familiar styles for your work, and you will come to understand all the problems these documentation styles actually solve for you—problems that, right now, you probably could not even imagine. For now, you mainly need to remember that they are meant to be used precisely, and that their accurate use is your best method to avoid charges of plagiarism.

## Avoiding Plagiarism

Certainly, you understand that you cannot have someone else do your writing for you or copy a paper and turn it in as your own. Most students also quickly understand the point of the Grand Valley policy forbidding submission of the same work in two different classes (including earlier high school classes)—at least unless you have permission from both instructors. Many first-year college students believe that as long as they avoid such extremely dishonest behavior, they cannot be accused of plagiarism; unfortunately, that belief is not correct.

Plagiarism is not simply a matter of dishonest intentions. Working with research sources requires writers to understand difficult aspects of plagiarism and make skilled, positive efforts to credit sources accurately and fully. Again, everyone knows that you cannot use the words of other writers without putting those words in quotation marks and giving the original writer credit. Many first-year students are surprised to find that, to avoid committing plagiarism, they also must do the following:

- Give credit to sources for their information and ideas as well as their words;
- Quote any exact phrases from the source, even if only a few words at a time, when they are included within your own sentences;

- Avoid using the same general sentence structure used by the source, except in exact and clearly marked quotations;
- Use your documentation style precisely to make perfectly clear when you are using material from a source and when you are presenting your own words and ideas.

In WRT 150, we expect students to learn more about documentation and avoiding plagiarism as the course goes on, so we may continue to work with your drafts even if they contain sections that might commit intentional or unintentional plagiarism. If you want more information about why we do that, read the statement by the national Council of Writing Program Administrators (CWPA) about best approaches to working with students on the concept of plagiarism, found online at http://www.wpacouncil.org/positions/WPAplagiarism.pdf.

Furthermore, we may not always see when you are using material from sources while we are working on your drafts. We rely on you to inform us of that. Nevertheless, by the end of the course, in your final portfolio, we will check closely for plagiarism and hold you entirely accountable for it according to the Grand Valley Student Code. Thus, you need to be sure that you understand how to document all your sources before the end of WRT 150. Be sure that you ask your teacher or consultants in the Writing Center about any instances of possible plagiarism in your work.

## WRT 150 Student Resources

### Computer Classrooms

While we do use other schedules and plans, WRT 150 classes generally meet twice a week, once in a traditional classroom and once in a computer classroom. Computer classrooms are sometimes used simply for writing and revising drafts, but your instructor may introduce a range of activities—brief in-class writing exercises, peer review sessions, and research assignments, for example—to help you gain expertise in a range of writing skills and strategies.

Any Grand Valley computer that you use in a computer classroom gives you the option to save items to a personal drive (the "N" drive), also known as your network account. You can access items saved to your network account from various campus locations, such as other campus computer labs and some campus living quarters, as well as from other Grand Valley campuses. You can also retrieve items on the N drive from an off-campus home computer. Seek assistance from Grand Valley's IT office (331-2101) for more information about file transfer.

The computer classrooms use recent versions of Microsoft Word, which is different from Microsoft Works, as the primary word-processing software. This means that Microsoft Works documents and some other documents do not open in a computer classroom unless you have saved them in a compatible format like rich-text format (.rtf), which you can do with nearly any word processing program. It also means that documents prepared in the computer classroom will not open on some other computers, especially older computers, unless you have saved them in rich-text format or another format used on that computer. Your teacher may be able to suggest other programs and methods for working on the same files both at home and in a computer classroom.

## The Library and Online Library Resources

The goal of library-related instruction in WRT 150 is to help you become an information-literate lifelong learner who can use academic and professional research methods and sources. In order to reach this goal, you will learn how to develop and implement a research strategy, locate the resources necessary to meet your information needs, and evaluate the information that you find.

Many WRT 150 teachers work closely with Grand Valley librarians and bring librarians into class to help you learn how to use Grand Valley's libraries and online library resources. In addition, each class has a designated library liaison who will work with you on your research for WRT 150. Ask your teacher for the name of your library liaison, or feel free to ask library staff to help you find the right person. Many first-year college students do not understand that librarians in a college research library are eager and ready to offer substantial help to you, both in conducting your research and in learning how to become better researchers. Grand Valley's librarians are also faculty members who serve as part of our teaching staff. Ask for their help.

## The Fred Meijer Center for Writing

Peer writing consultants work in all of the writing center locations as well as in WRT 098, WRT 150, and WRT 305 classes and in computer labs. Consultants do not simply check grammar and mechanics or guess what grade a paper may receive, but they do provide helpful feedback, offer advice, model writing strategies, and ask questions in order to help students improve as writers. Essentially, the role of a consultant is to provide a well-trained pair of eyes to help writers think more critically about their own writing, and to assist writers in devising a plan for revision.

Most WRT 150 teachers use computer classrooms for consultations. In that setting, students have instant access to a consultant. Since consultants are trained across the board, they can discuss any issue that may arise while you are working through writing activities or drafting and revising your papers. For example, you might need a quick discussion about the purpose of topic sentences, a guided tour through the library's many online resources for research, or a more in-depth conference about a whole draft. Make a point to seek out your writing consultant often. When you establish a working relationship with your writing consultant, he or she will come to understand your unique writing strengths and challenges, and can offer advice that is useful for the specific purposes you have in mind for your writing projects.

Consultants also sometimes help to lead small-group discussions in WRT 150 classrooms. Small groups serve as a place to cultivate ideas, mold them into new shapes, and devise a plan for a paper. The consultant's role in these situations is to help the group stay on track, encourage everyone's involvement in the discussion, model or prompt the group to use effective feedback strategies, and offer another perspective on your writing.

Here are some tips for making your group discussions work:

- Come prepared with specific questions or areas of your writing for which you need feedback.
- Bring enough copies of your draft for each student and the consultant to have one. This allows your readers to follow along and write comments on the papers, which you might find helpful later

in your revision process.

- Solicit the advice of everyone in your group, not just the writing consultant. The more readers' ideas you have, the better idea you have about whether your writing is working.

In labs or small-group discussions, consultants are there as a resource to work through your individual writing needs. Get to know your classroom consultants early in the semester, and consider visiting them outside of class, too, when they are on duty in the writing center.

of Writing

Department

# W Portfolio Grading FAQ: Questions You Might Have

**1. Why is a group of Writing 150 teachers reading my papers and determining my final grade rather than just my own teacher?**

A group of four to seven teachers (including your teacher) has been reading samples of your class's writing throughout the semester to discuss and agree about what is an A, B, C, D, and F paper. The goal of the instructors in the group is to set fair and accurate grading standards. The standards will develop after discussing samples from your class and other classes throughout the semester. This agreement between two Writing teachers will constitute the bulk of your grade.

**2. Does my teacher have any say as to what grade I get on my portfolio and what grade I receive in this class?**

Yes. Your teacher will always be one of at least two portfolio readers of your work at the end of the term. If the second reader in the group agrees with your teacher about the grade for your portfolio, then that agreement will determine the grade you receive on the portfolio. If the second reader does not agree with your teacher, then a third reader will be asked to read your portfolio. If the third reader agrees with your teacher, then the grade stands. If the third reader agrees with the second reader, then your grade is based on the agreement of readers two and three. The goal is to arrive at a "community" grade rather than a grade based solely on one teacher's preferences.

**3. What happens if one person in the portfolio group grades much harder than the others? Doesn't this mean I'll probably get a low grade if that person reads my portfolio?**

No, not necessarily. If the second reader does not agree with your teacher, a third reader is asked to read your portfolio and decide which of the first two readers is closest to the standards that the portfolio group has agreed about during the semester. (See question #2.)

**4. I think each teacher should grade his or her own students' work.**
Each teacher does have a hand in grading their students' work, but the
portfolio groups assure students that their grades are a reflection of community standards—departmental and university-wide.

**5. How can the portfolio group grade my papers if they haven't seen the
assignment?**
Writing 150 is a course that is designed to give you practice and instruction in the various kinds of writing that you will be asked to do throughout
college. The portfolio group therefore wants to be general in their assessment of your writing. They want to look at three samples of your writing
and describe the group of three as "excellent," "good," "average," or "below
average or failing." The ideal is that this grade reflects what most professors
would say if they picked up your portfolio and read it. We want your grade
to be based on the general quality of your writing alone, not on how well
the writing satisfies teacher-specific instructions.

**6. My teacher said that I have to type single space, have fewer than two
sentence fragments, and underline the thesis statement in every essay just
to get a C. If the portfolio group doesn't know this, then what happens?**
Teachers often have "minimum requirements" that they want every paper
to meet. For example, some say that a paper can't be handed in more
than one day late. When teachers have such requirements that may not be
the same as other teachers in the portfolio group, they will enforce those
requirements by making sure you meet them before you submit a portfolio to the portfolio group at the end of the term. This way, everyone who
reads your portfolio will assume it has met any teacher-specific minimum
requirements. If you don't meet minimum requirements that your teacher
sets, your teacher won't allow you to submit a portfolio at the end of the
term.

**7. Could two people in my portfolio group agree that I deserve a B and
then my teacher give me a C anyway because of absences or class participation?**
The portfolio grade is the "bulk" of your grade for the semester. Typically
you should not expect your grade to be adjusted by your teacher beyond
a plus or a minus for the grade the portfolio group (which includes your
teacher as first reader) gives you. If your grade needs adjusting down a
whole letter grade, you probably didn't meet the minimum requirements

(e.g. too many absences) and you should not have been allowed to submit a portfolio in the first place and been given an F. If a teacher over in Biology looks up your grade in WRT 150, they should be assured that this grade basically reflects how well you write, not your attendance, your improvement, or your good (or bad) attitude.

**8. Just looking at my portfolio at the end of the term doesn't show how much I've improved. Shouldn't my grade be based, at least in part, on my improvement?**
No. Your grade in WRT 150 should be based on the quality of your writing at the end of the term. This way, what counts as A, B, C, D, or F is the same for every student, or at least as close to being the same as we can manage. Teachers can adjust grades (usually with a plus or a minus) based on your participation, improvement, or other factors.

**9. I like to have grades during the semester so that I know how well I am doing. I don't want my grade at the end of the term to come as a big surprise.**
We agree. Your teacher should be reading your writing throughout the semester and responding to it with comments, personal conferences, endnotes, and suggestions for revision. Most 150 classes have tutors from the Writing Center that work with you and point out strengths and weakness in your writing. And many teachers will have you read and comment on other students' work.

For most students, a grade is not necessary for early drafts because the proper focus is on what the paper could be, not on what it is. But if you want a grade on an assignment and your teacher has not given one, just ask. The teacher will be able to tell you where she thinks the paper falls within the range of A to F. The teacher will probably tell you what she and others in the portfolio group have been saying about writing like yours. Don't be surprised if the teacher says, for example, that some in the group might say C and she, or others in the group, might say B. Group members often disagree, especially early in the semester, about what is an A, B, and C. If the teacher says your paper is probably a low B or a C, your next question should be: "what could I work on in this paper that would improve it?" Your teacher should love this question and this should give you the feedback you need to feel encouraged to try to make even a good paper better.

**10. It seems to me that the portfolio-grading system is all about judging final products. I thought we were supposed to be interested in the writing process?**

At GVSU we use portfolios as "grading groups" to respond to the need to develop community standards and to respond to the University's desire for a "check" on how well students can write before they move on to the upper-level courses. One aim (there are others) of the portfolio system is to protect students from being misled by "easy" graders and being treated unfairly by "hard" graders. Nevertheless, our composition program is very much concerned that you are learning strategies and skills that help you develop your own writing process.

In fact, because the portfolio group grading system focuses on what you can do at the end of the semester as represented by your portfolio, it encourages and gives opportunity for every paper (except for the in-class paper) to be revised. Revision is the heart of the writing process. That is, we teach and value better writing processes because they do tend to produce better writing. In the end, we believe that grading your results keeps the best focus on learning to use writing processes effectively.

**11. The portfolio group read my paper but didn't give me feedback. Why not?**

The portfolio groups do their evaluation after the course is over and are only concerned with grading. Your teacher is part of your portfolio group and his or her feedback on your paper throughout the term should be counted as feedback from the portfolio group. Your teacher is helping to set standards in your portfolio group, so listen closely when your teacher comments on your papers. It is your teacher's job to give feedback and help on your writing during the term. If you aren't getting it, ask again. Also, don't overlook the value of getting help from the writing tutor and the other students in your class.

**12. What is supposed to be in my portfolio?**

Every student should submit three papers, including at least one with citations and references that show your ability to conduct scholarly research and use its results effectively. Ask your teacher if you are not sure. Your teacher and the other students should help you make good choices about what goes in the final portfolio.

### 13. Can I include a paper in my portfolio from another class?

No. All papers in your portfolio must have been assigned and seen by your teacher. Students who submit work from another class or work that is not his or her own violate the Student Code's provisions on academic honesty and integrity, a very serious matter. The results may include failing the course and being reported to the Dean of Students for further action.

# Good Writing in WRT 150

When we set out to choose portfolios to be published in this handbook, we don't try to anticipate which ones will serve as perfect models for future students. So what are we looking for when we begin the portfolio selection process? Our goal is to select writers who understand their papers' purposes, know what it is they are trying to accomplish in their work, and we look for authors who keep their audience in mind as they write. No matter what your assignment may be, the keys to good writing remain consistent—a solid sense of purpose, focus, and audience. But there are many portfolio essays that meet these requirements that are submitted for possible publication, so we try to choose pieces from writers that tackle diverse subject material. In showcasing work from previous WRT 150 students, we hope to open up classroom dialogue about the content as well as the writing. We have chosen six writers to showcase in this year's edition of the book and each has something special to offer.

In **Portfolio One**, Alison Village actively engages college-level readers with her well-thought out topics and sophisticated writing style. In "Rules of the Bush" Alison vividly recounts her interviewee's insatiable appetite for canoeing in the wilds of Northern Canada. Her descriptive language enables the audience to feel the deep solitude of the outdoors, visualize the haunting glow of the aurora borealis, and experience the unparalleled rush of plunging into whitewater rapids. The amazing voyage almost ends in tragedy except for a guardian angel protecting the pair from physical harm and allowing them to escape their wilderness adventure alive. Her second essay "The Necessity for Proactive Opposition against Ecological Impact of Invasive Species on Native Ecosystems" investigates how the Great Lakes have been invaded by non-native species like zebra mollusks, lampreys, round gobies to the ire of environmentalists, sportsmen, and politicians alike. Village uses her own first-hand account to highlight the devastation that can occur on a local level when an invasive species moves into an ecosystem and becomes a dominant fixture in a shockingly short period of time. She effectively develops this focus by utilizing significant discussion, details, and examples within her paper. The focus of the text is critical because it informs readers what territory the writer plans to cover and allows the writer to shape his or her writing into a coherent, unified work. Alison ends the portfolio with "Bird's the Verb," which chronicles her beloved birding hobby and how it has made her into who she is today. Village cleverly crafts her essay in such a way that it makes readers look forward to learning how this pastime allows her to travel, meet new people, and inspires her to become more environmentally responsible. Alison's eye for detail and precise use of language makes her sentences easy and pleasurable to read.

**Portfolio Two** by Benjamin Andrus begins with a personal narrative "Citizen Warrior" about coming to terms with going to war abroad and then facing terrorism on the home front. He poignantly captures witnessing the worst mass shooting ever to take place on an American military base and reflects upon its devastating aftermath. He discovers, like many military personnel, that the transition from citizen to warrior and back again is a complex and challenging process. Andrus' second paper "Ergo Bibamus" contends that beer, from the earliest hunter gatherers to modern times, has been the driving force behind not only these aspects but everything that makes humanity what they are. His philosophical piece clearly demonstrates his ability to set up and incorporate information from pertinent outside sources in a manner that is purposeful. Letting your reader know exactly which authorities you rely on is an advantage: it shows that you have done your research and that you are well acquainted with the literature on your topic. He also successfully integrates his own ideas with those of other scholars. Benjamin's final essay "Traditionally Unprepared" explores how students who typically attend college right after high school graduation are not completely prepared to deal with the academic or social challenges that college presents. Once again, Andrus clearly demonstrates his information literacy skills and his keen ability to use university-level academic research as a way to more fully develop his ideas as a writer. Andrus also consistently maintains a professional tone in each of his portfolio papers.

Kamara Bailey begins **Portfolio Three** with "Marbleized," a moving memoir about how family recipes can keep our heritage alive and evoke vibrant memories of our relationships with family members who are no longer with us. Bailey elegantly conveys how food reminds us of experiences long forgotten and lets us relive feelings of comfort, satisfaction or excitement.

Preserving her Aunt Beth's special recipes allows her to access these emotions any time she chooses. Next, Kamara profiles Grand Rapids' homeless in "The Community of Homelessness, providing an intimate glimpse into what it takes for individuals to truly live without a home. By conducting her own primary research, Bailey is able to discover something unexpected and add to the body of knowledge surrounding her topic. In addition, well-written paragraphs, like hers, display clear logic; they have a tight structure that leads the reader through the development of its content. In her last piece "Red-Ribboned Selection" Kamara covers another compelling social issue—the increasing number of families in the U.S. who are devoted to adopting an HIV positive child. She notes that although educational, medical, and legislative advances explain, in part, the increasing adoption of HIV infected children; there are also more personal reasons why families are choosing these children to adopt. Bailey personalizes her essay a bit more by sharing her sister and brother-in-law's own journey to adopt a child who is HIV positive. Readers enjoy portfolios like Kamara's because they offer an interesting interpretation or perspective that gives them something interesting or provocative to respond to.

Connor Klunder's use of solid sentences, clear word choice, and effective structure makes **Portfolio Four** a great example of strong academic writing. In "Helmet Law Hostility" he successfully argues the value of instituting a nationwide helmet law by supporting his various points with valid evidence. In scholarly writing, student writers need to make some sort of claim and use evidence to support it, and their ability to do this well separates their papers from those of students who see assignments as mere accumulations of fact and detail. In "Using Insurance Justly" Klunder investigates the increasing number of insurance fraud cases and questions how effective the current solutions really are. Connor does more than just summarize information that he has gathered. He is able to develop a point of view on or interpretation of the research and provide evidence of his position. Klunder wraps up his portfolio with "Learning about Unemployment" where he discusses America's current economic recession and how it should be dealt with. This paper, like the others in this collection, is purposefully organized and substantially developed with supporting evidence, examples, and reasoning. Readers can easily see how the order in which information appears supports the focus and purpose of the papers. Conner's papers also highlight understanding a writing assignment as a series of tasks, including finding, evaluating, analyzing, and synthesizing appropriate primary and secondary sources

**Portfolio Five** by Claire Norman begins with a profile of an "ordinary" sixteen-year-old girl named Jordyn Wieber with an "extraordinary" talent and her "not-so-typical" coach John Geddert. We get a detailed account of how hard the two work to reach Jordyn's dream of being a world renowned gymnast. Her essay is both entertaining and readable because she weaves in bits of colorful descriptions, energetic anecdotes, and fascinating quotations. Claire's language also comes across to the audience as both mature and purposefully controlled. In "Riding like a Girl" Norman's title and introductory paragraphs swiftly inform readers of the paper's topic, purpose, and focus that make us look forward to reading further. Effective pieces of writing have a defined focus and a clear vision that orders what is being said. Without a clear focus, writer's stories or essays degenerate into lists of loosely related events or facts with no central idea to hold them together, leaving the reader to ask "so what?" Claire's final essay "Man and the Missile" is an introspective reflection on the existence of nuclear missiles and their impact from a personal and global perspective. While she dreams of world peace, the reality is that the U.S. may never see a world free of nuclear missiles. However, what Claire can see is a reduction in the mass number of nuclear missiles throughout the world. As a writer, Norman consistently anticipates the needs and expectations of her readers in order to convey important information and argue for a particular claim— in this case the need for nuclear disarmament. In closing her essay, she asks us to talk to our friends, family members, and local representatives about fighting for a decrease in nuclear missiles. Conclusions are the part of the paper that will most likely linger longest in your reader's mind. Norman's concluding thoughts remind us to leave readers with a poignant idea or a sense of why what they read was so important.

In **Portfolio Six** Loyd Webb opens with "A Golden Experience" that profiles Robert Shangle and his performance art piece *Under Construction*. A West Michigan native, Shangle performs as a live statue at such venues as Art Prize and the LivingStatue World Championship. Through interviewing Shangle, we learn firsthand how he is both an artist and an art form. He also uses photographs in his appendix to visually showcase his topic further. Readers appreciate such works because Loyd has attended to surface-level features to make it conform to readers' expectations of style, grammar and usage, and manuscript conventions. His focus on words, phrases, and sentences promotes not only correctness but also precision and rhetorical effectiveness. In "Eye on the Prize" Webb discovers how he, not his eye condition is holding him back from meeting his true potential. His effective use of dialogue and the narrative's clearly defined significance allows us to understand why he wrote it. Ask yourself, why do you want to tell this story? Think about the reasons for your choice and how they will shape what you write. The final piece "Manual Mutiny" discusses the Diagnostic and Statistical Manual of Mental Disorders (DSM) and how it has attracted controversy in the field of psychology. Loyd argues the DSM is a reckless expansion of the diagnostic system, lacks scientific rigor, and excludes some mental health professionals' contributions to diagnosis and treatment of patients. Webb's persuasive essay flows effortlessly and makes sense from the order of his ideas to his individual sentences. In order for the ideas to make sense, there must be an overall purpose behind them— that is, you must have clear intentions and reasons for writing what you write. This purpose should go even deeper, that is, your individual sentences and sometimes even words alone should serve a specific purpose. Webb, like the other student writers in this collection, had strong portfolios that possess clear purposes and single focuses.

We invite WRT 150 instructors and students to read and discuss these six portfolios as a way to generalize about what characterizes good writing in the first-year writing program at Grand Valley State University. As you read, notice the similarities and differences from portfolio to portfolio— the kinds of writing included, the number and types of sources cited, the length of the papers, and so on. Keep in mind that hundreds of other students wrote quality portfolios last fall and winter, and although they were probably as diverse in subject material as the essays exemplified here, all the writers understood the keys to good writing—composing with a solid sense of purpose, focus, and audience.

Alison Village
WRT 150

## Rules of the Bush

### As told to the author by Dan Rachor

Water dripped from my cuffs as I stood knee-deep in the frigid eddy, the river's roaring tumbling through my senses. Our gear, hastily flung on the shore in colorful disarray, settled into the sphagnum carpet. An intensifying drone emanated from the surrounding forest as squadrons of mosquitoes gravitated towards the smell of sweat and blood, enveloping my head net in search of a penetrable gap. My thoughts, assailed by the icy current, the maddening whine, and the precariousness of our situation raced without logical direction. Up until this moment, my paddling partner had never been one to mince words about his lack of faith; now, he stood in the river beseeching the living God to provide a rescue from our predicament. I had rarely felt so incapable, so inexperienced...so *alive*.

I have been plagued with an insatiable appetite for Canoe Country since I was a young boy. The rivers, once the major interstates of indigenous North Americans, then the French-Canadian fur traders remain wild, tumbling, largely unknown corridors that slice through granite hills and squalid bogs. It is rough country, far from civilization and not for the faint-of-heart or careless; a hastily-made mistake could reap disastrous results. Spending a month following the misty trails of the voyageurs and encountering only one or two parties of equally adventurous paddlers is not uncommon. However, the solitude you feel when you fall asleep on a rock beneath flashing aurora borealis, the eagerness tempered with caution as you plunge into a chute of whitewater – the accomplishment you feel as you ease your canoe and fifty-pound pack off your shoulders after a two-kilometer struggle up rocky hills and through treacherous swamps – it's simply unrivaled.

So, I have committed to an annual date of dancing the swifts of these captivating boreal waterways. Late July is when I make good on this promise. Southern Michigan is a steamy mess of heat, humidity, and exponentially growing lawns–and the magnetic pull of the north drags me in a wild venture towards the relative cool that lies north of the fortieth parallel. Icy whitewater replaces tepid lakes, broadleaf trees give way to pungent, impenetrable stands of spruce, and rules of civilization become irrelevant

---

*Alison wrote her portfolio in the class of Professor Craig Hulst.*

under the unforgiving rules of the Bush. It's that time of year when gold-eneye ducklings on beaver ponds fall prey to gaping muskellunge, when opportunistic black bears ravage abundant, sweet, wild blueberries – and, if you're unlucky, your own food cache. Most importantly, the black flies' voraciousness has ebbed.

Soon, this year's edition of Canadian yearnings had morphed into real-ity. Fourteen hours of driving–and I'm no trucker–had taken its toll, so we'd set up camp on the highway's deserted shoulder. Gear that had been so painstakingly organized in the back of my van was now jumbled mayhem from our frantic set-up in a race against waxing mosquitoes and waning daylight. We were a mere forty kilometers from the outfitter that would fly us to our put-in the next morning, and anticipation was high as we drifted to sleep under the eerie caroling of loons.

The next morning, I walked around the float plane, checking that my brand new royalex canoe had been properly secured underneath. Satisfied, I climbed into the machine, followed by my bow paddler Dwayne and then the bush pilot. It was a short, uneventful flight over the roiling gorges we would soon be paddling; our already peaking anticipation soared. We soon were on the ground, cataloging our gear–bear barrels, tents, water filters–all the necessities for a week in the bush. This would be my fourth whitewater river, putting me at that dangerous stage between inexperience and compe-tence where overconfidence lurks, coloring caution and judgment.

My previous trips had been in my trusty solo canoe, but the tandem was a new acquisition; getting used to paddling in rhythm with another would be a new experience. Since I didn't know many people up to a week-long plunge into the wilderness, I had settled for a partner, Dwayne, whose paddling prowess had yet to be determined. In fact, Dwayne was simply the husband of a woman who I had recently baptized into my Seventh-day Adventist congregation. Because Dwayne was not a Christian, perhaps his wife had sent him on a trip with me, a pastor, in hopes of a transformation – for I don't know many women who push their men to participate in an activity where the slightest mishap could reap disastrous results. Regardless of his paddling inexperience, I was grateful to have a partner . . . and just his willingness to go spoke volumes for his desire for adventure, something necessary of anyone about to venture into the wilderness.

I gently set our cherry-red canoe into the clear shallows of walleye-filled Lac Dumoine and then eased my weight onto the wicker seat. I turned and asked, "Dwayne, do you mind if we have a word of prayer before heading out?" He shrugged his shoulders, so I thanked God for the privilege to enjoy His creation, asked for wisdom as we set off, and requested that He oversee our safety. I silently prayed that Dwayne would be able to see Christ through me, and that I would be able to share my faith in a tactful manner. Soon, my wooden paddle skimmed the surface, the swirls of displaced water propelling us forward as Dwayne and I reached in unison for the water. However effortless it may be, flatwater paddling lacks the technical challenge that rapids provide, so I eagerly strained to feel the slightest tug of current that would let us know that we'd reached the gateway of the turbulent Dumoine.

The Dumoine River is only 129 kilometers long, yet drains an impressive 5380 square kilometers (Campology). The sheer amount of water pounding through its relatively short span results in a very strong current and frequent, significant rapids. Rapids, consisting of fast water funneling you toward protruding obstacles, abound on northern rivers. Rocks reach up, scathing the bottom of your boat, demanding a toll paid in canoe paint as if they're trying to prevent your passage to the deep, trout-filled pools ahead. I have occasionally found the carcass of a canoe lying abandoned on the shore skirting a rapid, serving as an important reminder of the strength of rushing water.

Rapids dictate respect from even the most experienced paddler, for recklessness could lead to loss of supplies, loss of your boat, or even loss of life. The horror felt when your boat grinds into a rock and swings sideways, filling with water as the river rushes in and claims your gear is just as intense as the adrenaline thrilling through your body after a successful run. Therefore, the deciding factor of how you will exit the rapid relies on the meticulousness with which you read the rapid from shore. Is it runnable? If not, do we have to portage, or can we line the canoe and walk it through the treacherous spot? Is that bulge a boulder or a harmless haystack formed by fast water slamming into still water? And if it's a haystack, is it big enough to rush into our boat and swamp us?

Soon after we entered the river, our bow was pointed towards the approach of Birch Rapids, an impressive class three set. The Bush rules dictated that we pull up on shore and plot our path, and we weren't in any position to argue. So, we picked our way along the rocky shore and analyzed the situation. We hurled rocks at potential haystacks, straining to hear the dull "thunk" as boulders posing as haystacks revealed their true identity. Finally, we tossed a branch into the current and watched the current flirt with it, knowing that our boat would want to follow the same path. Cautiously, we entered the rapid. We fought the current that toyed with our canoe, dragging us sideways towards obstacles then spitting us into tight chutes. We exhaled with relief when, mere seconds after our entrance, we hit the v-shaped exit where we rode down the frothing haystacks. Despite the rapid's challenging rating, I felt like our run had been executed well, and the rapids didn't present a problem.

However, Dwayne's inexperience was becoming apparent. He seemed unable to execute a draw, that stroke creating a pull of near gravitational magnitude between paddle and canoe. Drawing is a necessary component of safely running rapids, because when you're left at the mercy of swirling current thrusting your boat towards danger, you need a stroke that will move the canoe quickly – and drastically. In addition to his inability to draw, Dwayne was a large man. Consequently, he was unable to conform into correct rapid-running form of kneeling in the bottom of the canoe. This presented its own set of problems – in addition to keeping one's weight low and providing for more leverage, kneeling allows the stern paddler to have a better view of what the boat is being swept into. Although it's generally the bow paddler's responsibility to be the spotter, because of Dwayne's inexperience, I felt better when I was somewhat aware of what we were approaching.

Shortly after our first rapid, we met up with two French-Canadians. These heavy-drinking, jolly, and experienced paddlers were reminiscent of early furtraders, and we fondly christened them the "French Army". Although we were unable to converse, we leap-frogged with them for the next few days, and it was somewhat reassuring to know that someone else was on the river. Our third evening out, Dwayne, myself, and the French Army camped close enough to hear the roar of a rapid that we would read the next morning. Our excellent guidebook, *Rivers of the Upper Ottawa Valley*, recommended that we not attempt to run this rapid, and I was not inclined to since Dwayne's shortcomings turned even a lower-level rapid into a potentially precarious situation. And even though I had more experience than Dwayne, I was still a relatively naïve paddler and river reader. The next morning, however, the French Army, confidently approached this dangerous rapid, and ran a smooth, wide berth to the right, making it seem almost effortless, giving us false confidence. As the French Army rounded the bend in the river, we ignored the rules of the Bush and entered the rapid without first reading their path, following their strokes as closely as possible. Things seemed to be going smoothly until Dwayne – who was not kneeling – turned to me and casually mentioned, "There is a rock." Thinking it was just a "scraper" rock that would only claim some canoe paint before allowing us to proceed, I wasn't overly concerned.

I couldn't have been more wrong. A *boulder* loomed three feet above the river's surface shutting down hopes of further passage. "DRAW RIGHT!" I yelled, but it was too late. The current swept us into the rock, immediately swinging our boat sideways. I yelled at Dwayne to bail, and we leapt onto the boulder as the canoe crumpled under the pressure of the current.

I felt sick; the brand new canoe had cost more than a thousand dollars, and this money could have been used for church missions. And, we were now stranded fifty miles from nowhere and I was responsible for not only myself but also Dwayne. Fortunately, the current was holding the canoe against the boulder, and our gear, while wet, had not been lost. So, we struggled through the fast water to quickly toss our gear onto shore. I stood in an eddy, my thoughts mimicking its unproductive swirl, numbly feeling the water drip from my clothes. I was in shock, and all my senses were running on high speed. I knew our canoe wasn't coming out of the river, so we searched for a spot to set up camp – in my eyes, the only feasible solution. I felt responsible for Dwayne's wellbeing; this was his *first* wilderness trip, and *my* lack of foresight before entering the rapid had left us boat-less in a desolate area. Would Dwayne become even more skeptical about religion because he surmised that if I was a pastor and if there was a god, I would have some potent connection that could immediately get us out of this mess? I took a deep breath, gritted my teeth, and began videoing our canoe, thinking I'd at least have a good story to tell *if* we made it home. Then, I took a closer look at Dwayne. He was standing in the river, lips moving. I strained to pick words from the incomprehensible mutter. Dwayne was…*praying?!* After Dwayne's prayer, he muscled a tree stump from the shallows and approached the canoe. I was doubtful, but after a few moments of prying, the canoe popped from the boulder and I rushed to his side to help drag the mangled boat ashore.

We may have reclaimed our boat from the river, but it was folded nearly in half, rendering it of little use. I was certain the canoe was unsalvageable; however, we kicked and pulled at her frame and she suddenly popped into shape. Mere minutes after our brush with disaster, we were again headed down the river, shaken immensely.

The rest of the trip seemed to fly by; our extreme caution towards even the smallest riffle made the remainder of our float uneventful. Just before the Dumoine empties into the Ottawa River, it plunges through a beautiful, impassable gorge. At this final obstacle, we ran into two schoolteachers who spoke some English – the only other people we would meet on our trip. This outdoorsy couple had significant paddling experience, and acted shocked when we showed them the video of our canoe coming off the rock. They were in disbelief that we were still in the same boat.

As we dropped into the flatwater between that final chute and the Dumoine's mouth at the Ottawa River, I marveled about how our guardian angels had not only protected us from physical harm as we slammed into the boulder, but also provided us with the strength and intuition needed to retrieve and reshape our canoe. I still take that hardy canoe on wilderness float trips, and I never shy away from telling the story of how her dents and scrapes resulted from her nearly being put out of commission on her virgin voyage. As for Dwayne, well, he was baptized into my church about a year after our experience, although his wife never suggested he go on a float trip with me again.

## Work Cited

Campology. "Dumoine River." Web. 14 Nov. 2011.

Alison Village
WRT 150

The Necessity for Proactive Opposition against Ecological Impact of
Invasive Species on Native Ecosystems

The sun, angry red, creeps up the dull horizon as another day commences
at Pointe Mouillee State Game Area in southeastern Michigan. Wetlands
etching Lake Erie's shoreline erupt in cacophony as territorial Red-winged
Blackbirds, Marsh Wrens, and Common Yellowthroats add their voices to
the dawn chorus. Although Mouillee is a mere fragment of the magnificent marshes that once characterized Lake Erie, it encompasses well over
3,000 acres and is, in many respects, a fine example of a restored wetland
(USACE). In addition to being a haven for migrating waterfowl – and
sportsmen in their pursuit – Pointe Mouillee is a stronghold for many
species of rare marsh specialists whose presence in Michigan is tentative
(Chartier & Ziarno 119-125).

However, in recent times, Lake Erie, like the rest of the Great Lakes –
and for that matter, North America – has been the recipient of a barrage
of non-native invaders: zebra mollusks, lampreys, round gobies – species
whose very names elicit distress in environmentalists, sportsmen, and
politicians alike. While invasive species may not be the sole cause of any
given organism's decline, they certainly add another unnecessary pressure
to organisms already pressured by habitat destruction, climate change, and
pollution (Gurevitch and Padilla 471-473). These destructive intruders
have the jarring tendency of completely reforming previously healthy, pro-
ductive ecosystems into homogenous (and therefore inhospitable to biodiversity) expanses completely different from their original state. When even
one small part of an ecosystem gives way, diversity is lost, creating tentacles
of damage that unfurl expansively, jeopardizing other parts of the ecological community – and beyond. While the direct damage may appear to be
inflicted on the ecosystem, repercussions extend into economies dependent
on the function of that ecosystem, and in some cases, our very wellbeing
may become imperiled as diversity is lost (Reece et al 1240-1242). And, to
bring this sobering dilemma closer to home, invasive species are the leading
cause of biodiversity loss in the Great Lakes region! (Windle). Even though
taking a proactive stance on invasive species has tendencies to be more

successful *and* financially sound than dealing with invasive takeover as it occurs, little policy exists to allow this (Lodge et al. 2039, 2048). Invasive species are incredibly difficult to eradicate once they have been well-established. Rather than passively waiting for a problem to arise, then consequently struggling to eliminate it, we need to take measures to prevent the actual introduction of new invasive species.

It would be pertinent to provide a proper definition of an invasive species before delving too deep, so, without further ado, the National Invasive Species Information Center characterizes an invasive as an animal, plant, or pathogen that is "non-native (or alien) to the ecosystem under consideration and whose introduction causes or is likely to cause economic or environmental harm or harm to human health." (NISIC). Since invasive species no longer have their natural predators from the ecosystems they are indigenous to, conditions are optimal for them to reproduce exponentially. These conditions set invasives up to overthrow native species, and when this happens, the affected ecosystem undergoes drastic, typically negative change (Reece et al. 1242). Does this not rouse at least some concern? Because I have witnessed, first-hand, devastating results as an invasive species moves in to an ecosystem and becomes dominant in a shockingly short period of time, my heart always sinks when I see an invasive in a locale where they previously didn't have a hold, for I know what's to come.

Going back to Pointe Mouillee, many non-native organisms have assailed the marsh during the last few decades. By using the plant Purple Loosestrife (*Lythrum salicaria*) as specific example, I hope to establish the seriousness of allowing ecosystem takeover, so the necessity of proactivity for this scenario is realized. At Mouillee, the fine balance of a healthy marsh ecosystem has been imperiled by numerous non-indigenous species including the hardy *L. salicaria* (Hartig, Kauffeld, and Fuller 40). Like most aliens plants, this species proliferates at amazing rates, choking out native vegetation and rendering previously suitable marshes unfavorable habitat selection for many sensitive species.

Now a familiar sight in many marshes, L. salicaria arrived in North America from Europe during the early 1800s. The specifics of its influx are uncertain; evidence suggests that early settlers may have encouraged *L. salicaria* by cultivating it for its aesthetic appeal or reported medicinal qualities, or it may have come with ship ballast, a problem that still contributes to arrival of invasive aquatic species (Stackpoole 1). Regardless, it did not take long for *L. salicaria* to adapt to a new continent at such boundless rates that some early botanists thought it was a native!

To the unaware eye, *L. salicaria* is a stunning purple plant that readily colonizes wetlands and damp disturbed areas. Unfortunately, *L. salicaria* a huge problem because it has the tendency to choke out native vegetation, is not indicative of hosting most native species of birds, amphibians, and mammals, and is extremely hard to exterminate. In upstate New York, L.S. Smith noted in 1959 that, with time, invading *L. salicaria* ultimately overtook wetland habitats and rendered them impenetrable to even boats (Thompson, Thompson, and Stuckey). I have personally observed a channel between two small lakes get filled with *L. salicaria* to the point that only a canoe or kayak could get through, which compounded matters for local fishermen since there was no public launch on one of the lakes.

Why is *L. salicaria* so virulent? A healthy plant can produce more than two million seeds a year (Thompson, Thompson, and Stuckey). These seeds are primarily dispersed by water, but can also latch themselves onto fur, feathers, or mud that is attached to animals and humans. This means a muddy boat harboring *L. salicaria* seeds has the potential to transmit the noxious weed to previously untouched wetlands.

Once L. salicaria has been introduced, it does not take long for the affected marsh's composition to completely change. In New York's Montezuma National Wildlife Refuge, *L. salicaria* was observed as it overtook a wetland basin. In 1965, this basin contained native cattails and other desirable species – and *L. salicaria* was not noticed. However, in 1966, the loosestrife arrived. By 1968, it was solidly established, yet, accounting for not even five percent of the biomass of the basin, had not become a glaring problem. However, by 1978, *L. salicaria* had completely overthrown the balance of a marsh and accounted for ninety percent of the biomass (Thompson, Thompson, and Stuckey). As a result, plant diversity was drastically reduced, and since *L. salicaria* is not a particularly desirable species, many organisms would have consequently been forced to seek more suitable habitats, which in turn would render the affected wetland even less diverse.

If *L. salicaria* was a useful species, it likely would not be as significant of a problem. However, its stiff stems are inhospitable to most waterfowl species, and the plant, unlike those that it is choking out, is not a useful food resource for the vast majority of marsh dwellers. And, to add insult to injury, the dense mats of loosestrife provide cover for approaching predators. I have even seen *L. salicaria* alter a marsh habitat into a significantly more terrestrial state, due to the tendencies for its stems to collect silt and debris.

To provide a specific example of *L. salicaria* directly affecting a sensitive species, I'll cite the study entitled *Productivity and Nesting Habitat Characteristics of the Black Tern in Northern New York*. Black Terns, lithe freshwater marsh specialists, have long been designated a Species of Special Concern in New York (as well as in Michigan). Habitat degradation has been attributed as the major cause of their long-term decline, and *L. salicaria* is certainly not the sole component of their tentative future, but it appears to play a role. In the aforementioned study, Black Terns in a loosestrife-riddled wetland used only just over four percent of the available 8,000 hectare marsh – and none of that nesting occurred in areas where L. salicaria was present (Hickey and Malecki 583-585). Black Terns also suffered local extinction, or extirpation, at Montezuma National Wildlife Refuge, where they had formerly been common breeders. Not coincidentally, the timing of this extirpation corresponded to the population explosion of Purple Loosestrife, which spiked from covering nineteen percent to forty percent of the area (Blossey, Skinner, and Taylor 1789). This pressure on Black Terns is not an anomaly. Furbearing muskrats rely on cattails for food, which are choked out when loosestrife invades. Many studies have shown that waterfowl, uncommon vegetation, furbearers such as muskrats, amphibians – in short, most wetland residents – are negatively affected by Purple Loosestrife.

Unfortunately, as is the case with most invasives, managing *L. salicaria* is not a straightforward task. And, it *needs* to be managed, not only for the sake of benefiting native flora and fauna – but also so our fur-bearers and game birds can be sustained – which is, in turn, economically advantageous to *us*. Many of the possible methods of extermination – flooding, fire, replacement with other species, and herbicides – are more harmful to desirable fauna than to loosestrife. Two of the most-successful deterrents are relatively effective and safe – yet incredibly time-consuming and most effective when the patch has not been established (Stackpoole 3-4). Biological control, consisting of introducing a known predator from the invasive's natural range to the affected area, is an option in some cases – and introducing beetles from the genus *Galerucella* has been relatively successful in the control of *L. salicaria* at Pointe Mouillee (Hartig, Kauffeld, and Fuller 40). However, biological control involves introducing yet *another* non-native species into the ecosystem – and is this not the very situation being rectified? What can happen if this additional introduction is not host-specific, resulting in unforeseen harm that outweighs the benefits of biological control? Take for example Kudzu, federally listed as a noxious weed. It was initially introduced to prevent erosion resulting from faulty farming practices, but the Kudzu quickly engulfed everything in its path, creating serious problems for farmland and the timber industry. And, some of *Kudzu's* biological predators are also destructive to soybeans, so if that method of control had been utilized, a whole slew of problems could have resulted (Neofotis). It can be incredibly challenging to find a remedy that's not harmful to other species nor exceptionally laborious, yet still effective. Southwest Michigan Land Conservancy, an organization dedicated to preserving – and maintaining – the unique ecosystems of our state, has work bees for the sole purpose of removing the ubiquitous Garlic Mustard from its preserves. It's incredibly gratifying when one can finally see stunning native woodland flowers reappear on the forest floor – but pulling Garlic Mustard is a backbreaking, painstaking task – and it takes years for the mustard to finally cease growing back. If Garlic Mustard could have been prevented from taking hold in the first place, resources could have been more efficiently allocated.

Whether it's an exotic weed replacing native wetland plants, sea lampreys sucking the life from Lake Trout – and the Great Lakes fishing industry, or a miniscule invader from Asia rendering formerly magnificent stands of ashes condemned, invasive species are often extremely harmful to the surprisingly fine balance that our ecosystems have adapted to. And, they're exceptionally expensive to deal with. Invasive control costs the United States billions of dollars each year, and a significant chunk of those funds come from you, a taxpayer! (Lodge et al. 2036.) But, invasive *prevention* is a more efficient way of battling the problem. A significant recommendation to U.S. invasive policy management states that policy makers should attack invasion by emphasizing prevention, because "that is where the most cost-effective responses are possible: preventing organisms from being released or escaping alive." (Lodge et al. 2039.) So much money is spent on invasive extermination – but less attention is given to reducing new introductions, which means that those will have to be dealt with later, at potentially great financial – and environmental – cost (Lodge et al, 2041). I personally would be happy to support policy that meant a greater safeguard against new invasive species.

However, unless one is directly impacted by an invasive – and most of us are not – it's all too easy to turn a blind eye to the situation. And interestingly, a survey in Spain revealed that people were more willing for their money to be used for eradication, rather than prevention, of invasives (Garcia-Llorente et al. 430). One can sympathize with this logic, for if the problem in question is one of somewhat less visibility to the general public, why fix something that doesn't appear broken? My classmates who reviewed this very paper didn't recognize Purple Loosestrife by name, so I initiated an impromptu show-and-tell and pulled up a photo. Then, they realized that they'd seen Purple Loosestrife – but they had no idea that it was harmful, or even non-native! I surmise that this is a fairly accurate synopsis for my demographic, especially – so if non-scientists were better-educated about invasive species, would they be more willing to support preventative measures? One would think so.

These proactive procedures are not only much more economically efficient than trying to deal with the aftermath – they're more effective too. During a twenty-week period in Hawaii, the Department of Agriculture conducted unusually comprehensive inspections of imports. This effort uncovered significant numbers of non-native insects and pathogens that otherwise would have continued into improper ecosystems, with an estimated fifty percent of them becoming invasive! (Lodge et al. 2038, 2041.)

There are certainly barriers to introducing new policies to slow the spread of invasives – Phyllis Windle, in an appeal to various environmental agencies in 2003 cites lack of funding as an obstacle of establishing more complete policies targeting harmful non-indigenous species (Windle 2003); also, there are numerous agencies with little unification who have potential jurisdiction over invasives, making what policy exists confusing to enforce. I worked on a project this summer that involved multiple agencies at the state and federal level, and although there was certainly cooperative effort, there were plenty of frustrating idiosyncrasies between each agency.

These differences would be magnified with an issue as significant as invasive control.

Unfortunately, what little policy *does* exist is typically overly specific, applying, for example, to only *one* shipping channel (Lodge, 2048). Michigan actually has stricter regulations pertaining to invasive species than most Great Lakes states, but these laws do little good if the resources to enforce them don't exist (Kaminski-Leduc). In Michigan, conservation officers are the designated authority to deal with such laws, but our state encompasses 58,110 miles of land – and there are only approximately 230 sworn conservation officers at any given time (Library of Michigan; Michigan Department of Career Development).

As exemplified by *L. salicaria*, the sudden influx of non-native species makes it extremely difficult for native species to quickly adapt to their new surroundings. Care needs to be taken to prevent the introduction of new species – Purple Loosestrife, Sea Lampreys, and Emerald Ash Borers were not purposely introduced, by any means, but they still have played an exceedingly detrimental role in threatening biodiversity. As responsible individuals, it is our duty to ensure that we allocate sufficient resources in the fight against alien species. On a local level, we need to educate people on how they can prevent and slow the spread of non-indigenous species, and we can always contribute time to land conservancy work days oriented to removing invasives. Research that results in more comprehensive policy to control new, unintentional introductions needs to be supported, so that fewer invasives will become established and difficult-to-remove. And finally, we must ensure that there will be enough funds to enforce these policies. If we plan proactively, decades from now, duck hunters will still be able to simultaneously bolster Michigan's economy as they stalk their quarry in Pointe Mouillee's vast marshes.

## Works Cited

Blossey, Bernd, Luke C. Skinner, Luke C., and Janith Taylor. "Impact and management of purple loosestrife (Lythrum salicaria) in North America." *Biodiversity and Conservation*, 10 (2001): 1787-1807. Web. 24 September 2011.

Chartier, Allen T., and Jerry Ziarno. *A Birder's Guide to Michigan.* Colorado Springs, CO: American Birding Association, 2004. Print. 4 December 2011.

Garcia-Llorente, Marina, Berta Martin-Lopez, Paulo A. Nunes, Jose A. Gonzalez, Paloma Alcorlo, and Carlos Montes. "Analyzing the Social Factors That Influence Willingness to Pay for Invasive Alien Species Management Under Two Different Strategies: Eradication and Prevention." *Environmental Management* 48.4: 418-435. September 2011. Web. 4 December 2011.

Gurevitch, Jessica, and Dianna K. Padilla. "Are Invasive Species a Major Cause of Extinctions?" *TRENDS in Ecology and Evolution*, 19.9 (2004): 471-474. Web. 26 September 2011

Hartig, John, Jon Kauffeld, and Nita M. Fuller. *Detroit River International Wildlife Refuge Comprehensive Conservation Plan.* 2005. Web. 4 December 2011.

Hickey, Jeanne M., and Richard A. Malecki. "Nest Site Selection of the Black Tern in Western New York." *Colonial Waterbirds* 20.3 (1997): 582-595. Web. 24 September 2011.

Kaminski-Leduc, and Janet L. "Zebra Mussels."*OLR Research Project.* 2011. Web. 5 December 2011.

Library of Michigan. "Michigan in Brief." Web. 5 December 2011.

Lodge, David M., Susan Williams, Hugh J. MacIsaac, Keith R. Hayes, Brian Leung, Sarah Reichard, Richard N. Mack, Peter B. Moyle, Maggie Smith, David A. Andow, James T. Carlton, and Anthony McMichael. "Biological Invasions: Recommendations For U.S. Policy And Management." *Ecological Applications* 16.6 (2006): 2035-054. Print. 4 December 2011.

Michigan Department of Career Development. "#385 – Conservation Officer."*State of Michigan.* Web. 5 December 2011.

National Invasive Species Information Center (NISIC). "What is an Invasive Species." Web. 24 September 2011.

Neofotis, Peter. "Introduced Species Summary Project: Kudzo" *(Pueraria Montana).* 2001. Web. 4 December 2011.

Reece, Jane B., Lisa A. Urry, Michael L. Cain, Steven A. Wasserman, Peter V. Minorsky, Robert, and B. Jackson. *Campbell Biology.* San Francisco, CA: Pearson Benjamin Cummings, 2011. Print. 4 December 2011.

Stackpoole, Sarah. "Purple Loosestrife in Michigan: Biology, Ecology, and Management."*Michigan Sea Grant*, Bulletin E-2632. Web. 24 September 2011.

Thompson, Daniel Q., Ronald L. Stuckey, and Edith B. Thompson. *Spread, impact, and control of Purple Loosestrife* (Lythrum salicaria) *in North American Wetlands.* Washington D.C.: U.S. Dept. of the Interior, Fish and Wildlife Service, 1987. Web. 24 September 2011

U.S. Army Corps of Engineer (USACE). "USACE – Detroit District – Pointe Mouillee-Beneficial Use." Web. 4 December 2011.

Windle, Phyllis N. "Testimony to Joint Oversight Hearing, House Committee on Resources, Subcommittee on Fisheries Conservation, Wildlife and Oceans and Subcommittee on National Parks, Recreation, and Public Lands." *The National Environmental Coalition on Invasive Species.* 2003. Web. 4 December 2011.

Alison Village
WRT 150

Bird's the Verb

Setting: Saturday morning, 4 a.m. I descend from my precariously lofted bunk with the stealth of a lynx stalking a snowshoe hare, taking utmost care that my slumbering roommate remains undisturbed. Mission successful, I ease our door shut and slink into the abandoned hallway. A few moments later, I shove Robinson's lumbering door open, look for a flash of headlights, then slide into the waiting car and creep out of campus. A short drive later, we'll roll to a stop in a deserted parking lot, where I'll furtively unzip my backpack and pull out several thousand dollars' worth of goods.

But wait – suspicious as it sounds – what I'm doing is perfectly legitimate and legal, though the simple fact that I'm willingly alert at 4 a.m. *probably* classifies my behavior as deviant. And, this incongruity from the life of an average college student extends far beyond regular dark o'clock forays; on other days, you might find me wandering, binoculars in hand, around the most obscure corners of campus, or standing on a Lake Michigan dune, getting pelted by sleet. If one were to seriously stalk me, they'd find that I spend a ludicrous amount of time at, of all places, wastewater treatment plants and landfills!

Why? Since age six, I've identified myself with an eccentric, eclectic group of people – birders. According to Webster's dictionary, this means I am "a person who birds", with the verb "bird" being defined as "to observe or identify wild birds in their habitats" (Bird). My friends who have yet to cross to the dark side complain that I spend *too* much time looking for birds; I recently crowed to my boyfriend after making an identification that I've always struggled with, "Did you ever think you'd have a girlfriend that could pick a Thayer's [Gull] from the gull flock?!" I think we can safely deduce that Webster's definition accurately summarizes who I am.

However, while Webster suffices in giving a vague idea of what a birder might actually do, who we are extends far beyond the reaches of a nine-word account in some shelved, musty dictionary. And, contrary to a persisting, popular stereotype established by Miss Jane Hathaway of the Beverly Hillbillies and perpetuated by today's hordes of fanny-pack toting, floppy-hat clad women, birding isn't just an outlet for quirky old ladies to coo over baby geese. (Not that there's anything wrong with being a quirky old lady – or fussing over adorable, animate balls of yellow fuzz –that's the inevitable curse of being female…)

To contradict this label, the most serious, skilled, and dedicated (obsessive and insane?) birders I know are overwhelmingly male. A study emphasizing how gender affected birding tactics in North Carolina mirrors this perception; men were "significantly more active in their birding participation than women" (Moore, Scott, and Moore 94) and "reported being more skilled, had invested far more in equipment, got started at a younger age, and had watched birds longer." (Moore, Scott, and Moore 96). Although there are certainly many female birders, this same study found that they were "less compelled to focus on skill development and achievement than their male counterparts" (Moore, Scott, and Moore. 96). These findings align with my experience – women seem to approach birding in a more toned-down, less-competitive manner than men. And – go figure – I'm a woman who birds like a man.

So, gender may influence one's approach to birding, but what exactly does being a birder encompass? In a broad study undertaken by the U.S. Fish and Wildlife Service targeting birder demographics, birding was defined as an activity requiring "having taken a trip one mile or more from home for the primary purpose of observing [wild] birds" (U.S. Fish and Wildlife Service 4). Obviously, with an activity generating enough popularity that nearly a quarter of Americans participate to some extent (U.S. Fish and Wildlife Service 4), there will be significant disparity between birders' techniques. However, a big reason why birding appeals to such a diverse collection of people is *because* there are many different approaches to it.

One is the manner exemplified by the recent Jack Black and Owen Wilson movie *The Big Year*, where three men race around North America, demoting relationships, finances, and health in their frenzied attempt to get the biggest list of bird species within a year. I have birding friends whose approach mirrors The Big Year as they let birding become a religion of sorts. Somehow, the pursuit of a humble checkmark on a list rises above sleep, eating habits, and common sense in their personal hierarchy of needs. In the event that a difficult-to-find species shows up, they're not opposed to calling in sick, just so they can chase across the state – or, in extreme cases – country to chalk up another mark on the List.

Caleb is one of Michigan's most skilled birders and a good friend, and falls into the category outlined above. He lives in a landlocked county, where migration is mediocre at best. So, he spends hours engineering ways to maximize the yield. His latest idea? Spending hours in a lawn chair set in a flooded field, using decoys and recorded calls to lure shorebird species into range – species that he's seen time upon time outside the county. Kenn Kaufman, today a highly regarded identification expert, dropped out of high school in 1973. He hitchhiked across North America, subsisting on donating plasma and eating Friskies cat food. Why? So he could learn North American birds (Kaufman). I might have skipped out on a family funeral to see Michigan's eighth Common Ground Dove, *might* have exercised my powers of manipulation ("but Dad, by the time I have enough money to go to Nunavut, it's going to be extinct!") upon my parents so they'd drive me to New Jersey in pursuit of a quickly-declining arctic rarity, but I've since reformed my ethically questionable, fossil-fuel devouring ways. But while I don't necessarily advocate this type of birding, it's certainly there.

Then, there are individuals who might not be as obsessive about numbers on lists. Although they enjoy seeing new species, they prefer to combine birding with ecotourism. It's adventure-filled. It can be risky. It's a good way of bolstering struggling economies in a sustainable manner. Best of all, culture and fauna interweave like a Peruvian hammock; one night, the oppressive dark of an Amazonian jungle pierced only by the unearthly moan of a Great Potoo seemed to envelop me as I recalled my guide, Miguel's, tale from a few hours ago of how these large, nocturnal birds prey upon children's souls.

Yet others devote their time to becoming intimately acquainted with an area or species. Tim, always camo-clad and sporting a beard that would spark jealousy in Paul Bunyan, spends every spare moment (and then some) planted atop a dune (or, recently, out a few miles in a boat). Thanks to his efforts, I – and many others – now have a better grasp of the intricacies of migration on the Great Lakes. No matter the approach, the force driving it all can be likened to the almost primal urge of a hunter stalking their quarry, for the object of any birder is to *find birds*.

My own passion for birding caught fire one evening in April 1999. My dad griped, "I just washed the car yesterday!" as we bumped down a dusty road. Then, a lump nestled in a tree captured my attention. "Dad! *Stop!* I saw an *owl!*" He raised an eyebrow and kept driving. "Dad, go back there's an owl and I've never seen an owl and…" I trailed off, frustrated as any six-year-old faced with the onslaught of parental doubt. Fortunately, my mom looked back as the tree faded into the horizon. "Dave, go back. There actually *is* an owl." He threw our trusty LeSabre into reverse, and astoundingly, the owl didn't flush as we came to a stop below its perch. We spent the next half-hour reveling beneath the tawny Short-eared Owl's icy gaze, and it's just that simple: I was hooked.

My parents are not birders, so I'm still not quite sure what prompted them to suggest one afternoon that we "go look for ducks". However, I'm reasonably certain that they've regretted that decision ever since, because benignly "looking for ducks" quickly bourgeoned into an inescapable obsession. I spent hours with the Berrien Bird Club learning the behavior and vocalizations of the hundreds of species found in southwestern Michigan, took weekend trips to Whitefish Point Bird Observatory in the Upper Peninsula, and eagerly participated in citizen-science based surveys such as Christmas Bird Counts and Breeding Bird Atlases. Eventually, my hard work paid off as I made connections; I began to dabble with professional guiding and traveled to events geared for young birders across the United States. Incriminating as it is, I even met my boyfriend two years ago at bird camp.

It's been eleven years since the Short-eared Owl, and now, the "birder mode" switch has been forced into the "perpetually on" position. It's something I have little control of; just last week, I was walking to Pew Campus from Central Station, and, much to the amusement of the fishermen on the Fulton Street Bridge, I stopped dead in my tracks to appreciate a Peregrine Falcon barreling overhead. However, when I sling my binoculars around my neck, grab my scope, and consciously go birding, my approach is dependent on weather, season, and my mood. There are those blustery November mornings, the wind shaking my tripod and provoking a steady stream of tears – and southward-bound Red-breasted Mergansers – when I'll stand on a dune, keeping tally of every bird travelling south as I grimly persuade myself that a little suffering is worth better records of migration on the Great Lakes. Occasionally, I'll *find* an exceptionally out-of-range species, then gleefully enjoy the chaos it creates in those birders after a

Check on the List. Most of the time, my birding is relatively laid-back, consisting of nothing beyond casually navigating a woodland path accompanied, perhaps, by a friend and a bright vortex of foraging, singing warblers. Regardless of my approach, I always try to keep accurate notes of what I see, so that I can enter my sightings into eBird, a database dedicated to generating scientific data from citizen reports.

Birding hasn't simply been a precursor to my activities and career path, but through the formal study of, participating in conferences relating to, and simply enjoying birds, other birders and birding have significantly shaped me into who I am. Birding has given me many opportunities to travel, to meet new people, and to merely intensify my appreciation for intricate ecosystem relationships, which has in turn inspired me to be more environmentally conscientious. Because my favorite areas to bird are remote, I've been sucked into the joys of wilderness canoe and backpack excursions. Through presenting at birding events I've become a confident public speaker; sitting in a mosquito-infested Andean hillside photographing the little-known Crescent-faced Antpitta has taught me patience. And, of course, if it wasn't for birding, I'm sure that I wouldn't have found myself stranded by a landslide in the Ecuadorian Andes with two Spanish-speaking strangers for Christmas break!

I bird for the coursing thrill of satisfaction when I direct another birder until they too are fixated on a difficult-to-observe species. I bird for that moment when a burly jaeger flashes across my field of view in twisting pursuit of a gull, temporarily alleviating the misery of being battered by wind, sand, and sleet atop an icy jetty. I bird for those quiet mornings in my kayak, notebook in hand, as I document nesting of a state-threatened species in a tranquil wetland. I bird for the rosy-cheeked, scarf-bound joy of snowshoeing through a bog in subzero temperatures as I'm engulfed by a flock of tame, cheerful Boreal Chickadees. I bird for those evenings in early fall, when the sheer number of migrating birds create a green smear on the radar, inspiring me to lay out on a hill and feel completely miniscule and unimportant as thousands of indistinguishable flight calls mesh overhead. I bird for that moment in a deserted parking lot when I retrieve my binoculars from my backpack as I get psyched to get out there and *find birds*.

Works Cited

Kaufman, Kenn. *Kingbird Highway.* New York, NY: Houghton Mifflin Company, 1997. Print. 25 Nov. 2011.

"Bird." *Merriam-Webster.* Web. 20 Nov. 2011

Moore, Roger L., David Scott, and Annette Moore. "Gender-based Differences in Birdwatchers' Participation and Commitment." *Human Dimensions of Wildlife,* 13 (2008): 89-101. Web. 21 Nov. 2011.

U.S. Fish & Wildlife Service. "Birding in the United States: A Demographic and Economic Analysis." *U.S. Fish and Wildlife Service* (2006). Web. 14 Sep. 2011.

Benjamin Andrus
WRT 150

Citizen Warrior

Fort Hood, Texas; November 5th, 2009; 1:35pm, I was sitting in the Soldier Readiness Process Center medical building waiting my turn to see the case manager. The boredom was almost overcoming me, then suddenly, I heard firecrackers being set off near the front door. *What is this, some kind of drill? I really don't want to deal with this right now,* I remember thinking to myself. Screams pierced my eardrums and I shuddered with the realization that this was not a drill; this was not some elaborate war game. This was really happening. One of my fellow soldiers was now shooting at us with an automatic handgun. Hitting the floor, I tried to bury myself in the tile. I thought about my mom: how she used to make me soup when I was sick or how she would cry when she found out I was dead. I thought about my dad: playing catch in the back yard and listening to the Detroit Tigers on the radio while we shuffled through my new pack of baseball cards. Another firecracker string set off, and I jumped back to reality. *'Hail mary full of grace....'* I started praying.

From where I was packed against a crowd of other people trying to hide from the shooter, I could see other soldiers scrambling around the corner of the small dividers that separated the room. Some had blood on their clothes, some did not, but all of them had the look of dread. It wasn't until that moment that I finally realized what was going on. My mind kept trying to rationalize what was happening, but one of our own was now trying to kill us. *I am going to die, I am not going to leave this building,* was the only thing going through my head as the shooter walked around the room spraying more bullets into the huddled mass that we were. The blood of my comrades started to smear across the floor, and the group I was with had to crawl through it to reach the door. Looking to my left I saw the body of my fellow soldier laying face down in a pool of her own blood. *Why, why did he do this?* When the shooter exited the opposite side of the building we made a break for it, running like our lives depended on it. And they did. It is amazing how fast you can run when you are being hunted. *I am going pretty fast, I wish I could tighten my belt right now,* was my only thought. My mind was already throwing up walls, trying to make sense of what happened. I

---

*Benjamin wrote his portfolio in the class of Professor Emma Ramey.*

found other members of my unit and we piled into a van and drove back to our barracks.

To fully understand the extent of this horrible tragedy, let me take you back to 2003. I was a young man, only 21 years old, and had been a member of the U.S. Army Reserve for about a year. Standing in my apartment, in the middle of a grill out with a few friends, I was wondering why the girl I had a crush on did not show up. I just then noticed the Fed Ex envelope on the counter.

"When did this get here?" I asked

"This afternoon, sometime when you were asleep," came the reply from my roommate.

I worked third shift so sleeping through the best part of the day was part of my life. Ripping open the envelope, I pulled out the contents. Orders. From the army. "You are hereby ordered to report to Camp Atterbury, Indiana, no later than Dec 7, 0800hrs. 2003, for the purpose of Operation Iraqi Freedom."

My heart sank. My stomach made friends with my knees.

"I am going to war," I stammered. My mind was racing and all I could think of was *Black Hawk Down* and *Saving Private Ryan*.

"No, I don't think so, they probably just need you for training or something." My roommate didn't fully understand the significance of what being a soldier meant.

I was furious with his nonchalant attitude, and I felt I was being sent off to die in a desert and he was blowing it off. My heart was starting to catch up to my mind. It beat furiously trying to break free from my chest and save itself. Reading the orders again, something changed.

"We will see." I tried to be brave but my heart would not stop racing. I was scared.

Later that same year, I arrived to the mobilization site, scared and alone. All the new faces around me, the haunting idea of war passing unspoken between us. It was almost too much for me to handle. I could not, in my current state, wrap my head around the idea that I was going to war. It was all I could do to keep from crying into my pillow each night.

After a few weeks of training and refreshing all of us soldiers on our basic soldier tasks, we started to gel as a unit. Less and less did I find myself crying at night, and more and more we would hang out together and form bonds of friendships. The whole while, we all knew why we were there; but as the training intensified and the stress and pressure ramped up, we were able to lean on what we were learning and allow the uniform to take over. Bit by bit, I was transforming from a scared young man to a professional warrior.

I knew I was ready when I first saw the plane that would take my fellow soldiers and me to the desert. The fear, homesickness, and overall feeling of dread did not go away, but rather fuels the fire that is our uniform. We were soldiers, and in that moment I let my uniform take over. We looked each other in the eye and said, "If we are going to die in the desert, better us than our loved ones at home."

After a few months of being in Iraq, we settled down into a routine. Being fuel haulers, we were used to going on long missions brining diesel fuel to the far reaches Iraq. So one evening in late March, when we were told we had an early convoy and to prepare for being out almost a week, we didn't think much of it.

At 0430 the next morning we woke up and made our way down to the trucks to get them ready to go. My crew and I were working on our old hummer, which just got back from the maintenance shop after having some makeshift armor bolted onto the sides.

"Sgt. Driver[1], where are we going?" I asked after I just got done mounting and doing a functions check on my M249 SAW (Squad Automatic Weapon).

"Fallujah," he grinned.

"Isn't that like, kinda a hell hole right now?" I asked innocently.

"Yeah, the Marines need more fuel. So lucky us right?"

"Oh...well, lets do it." Same old missions, I felt fine.

At the convoy brief before we left, we decided the risk assessment was medium. And to a citizen driving non-armored vehicles through Bagdad to Fallujah in April of 2004 would entitle a little more than medium risk. To us, the transformation now complete, we thought of it as only slightly more dangerous than any other day.

We headed out, and not 50 miles from where we 'broke the wire,' gunshots rang out. The truck directly in front of where I was hanging out of the top of my Hummer exploded. Capt. Awesome, my platoon leader, called up to me. Leader

---

1. All the names used have been changed to protect the citizen warriors I fought with.

"Keep your eyes open. Contact right! Contact Right," He shouted.

'Contact right' was the soldier way of telling me that we were taking enemy gun fire from the right side of the vehicle.

"Don't worry laddie, there's plenty for the both of us. May the best dwarf win!" I shouted the *Lord of the Rings* quote, adrenalized, while whirling the turret to the right side and began to engage the targets.

"Andrus! Contact right, 2o'clock! 200 Meters!" Capt. Awesome's voice again rang out.

"Contact right. 2 o'clock. 200 meters. Confirmed!"

"Fire."

Even in these stressful and hectic circumstances we remained calm and followed the proper procedure. The transition went so smoothly and penetrated so deeply that we were totally consumed by the uniform. We were warriors now, and nothing could infiltrate the armor we built together back at the mobilization site.

When the transition is interrupted, or doesn't happen, things become disastrous.

Six years later, I was sitting with a group of other soldiers in the drill hall of Muskegon, Michigan. We all had received letters, ordering us to report to the unit, for deployment to Operation Iraqi Freedom. Looking over the people there with me, I could see the same looks in their face as I had in mine during the first deployment. When our platoon sergeant came in and told us that we were not actually going to Iraq, but to Afghanistan, a stunned silence fell on the room. The fear of the unknown crept back into my mind, as I remembered what this was like. I thought back to my predeployment days in 2003 and tried to be there for the younger soldiers.

Arriving at Ft. Hood, Texas, we all tried to put on our brave faces and jump into the training that would save our lives and prepare us for what was to come. The importance of this training was no mystery to me. I had been in this position before. I knew to lean on my fellow soldiers, be there for them and they would be there for me. We needed to create our bonds of friendship and build our defense before we flew out.

Halfway through my training, I had to go back to the Soldier Readiness Process Center medical building in order to clear up some paperwork that I was unable to finish when I went through it with my fellow soldiers. I was completely unprepared for what happened next. Looking back on what happened, I know that this single moment in my life has changed me more than anything else I have experienced.

The next morning, I found myself sitting on the cold ground of the close quarter's combat live fire range, battling a slight rain and harsh winds. My mind was on fire blazing through the shooting that happened to me the day before. Sergeant First Class Haven, the only other member of my unit in the room when the shooting broke out, was sitting with me.

"Can you believe they are making us do this?" he inquired.

He was quite a few years older than me, and I viewed him as a father figure. There was no one else I could talk to about how I was feeling or how I was dealing with the emotions that were threatening to cripple me. We talked about how we felt about having to continue our training.

"All I want is a day off. I mean how can I process this if I don't get the time? I am not doing that shit. I don't care what they do; I am not entering a building with other soldiers, that have loaded weapons, right now." I spoke with a false confidence trying to convince myself that I wasn't as mentally broken as I really was.

The ordered progression of my transformation from citizen to warrior was altered and broken. No one else in the unit, aside from Sergeant First Class Haven, knew what I was going through. The worst part of the whole process was that I had no one to support me. On the first deployment we all held up our shields, and like the Spartans holding at Thermopylae, we guarded each other and protected ourselves. Just as we were transitioning from everyday life, where the biggest problem is running out of eggs and having to make an unexpected trip to the store, to seeing one of the people that I would lean on, one of the people that was supposed to be encouraging me, one of the people who was supposed to be my brother in arms, one of the people that I counted on to not break that front we put up in the face of fear, take an automatic hand gun and start killing my fellow soldiers. Not only was I not expecting it, and not mentally ready for it, but I was betrayed.

I was alone.

Over the next few weeks the unit continued to prepare for deployment to Kandahar, doing all the necessary things to be cleared to leave the US. They took me to range after range, expecting me to play the war games as if nothing happened. I was expected to point my weapon at other soldiers and fire M.I.L.E.S. Gear, the Army's high tech version of laser tag, with blanks loaded in my weapon.

Every time I heard a gun shot my heart jumped. My commander did not give me any time off to reset my mind and manage what had happened. He kept pushing me into what I viewed as meaningless exercises to get ready to kill our enemies only days after I witnessed one of our own kill so many of us.

The day came and we all boarded the plane that was taking us to the desert. It felt like a dream, like a horrible nightmare I could not shake myself out of. Fear, homesickness, dread, loneliness, I was awash with emotions, none of them the same as my last deployment.

My roommate, and now best friend Private First Class Robinson and I were preparing for another trip at work on the base. We had been selected to do third shift logistical supply for Kandahar Air Field. That means we drove large amounts of supplies from the airstrip to the units that were stationed on the base. When we reached our destination, I tried to open up and talk to him about how I was feeling. I knew from my last deployment that I could not bear this burden on my own.

I turned off the truck and lit a cigarette. "It's hard to explain, I guess, like sometimes I can't sleep because I am thinking about it all the time."

"I don't know what to tell you." He hopped out and started undoing the straps on the trailer.

I played that over and over in my mind over the next few weeks. *I don't know what to tell you.* We were in two completely different places mentally. I wanted to be angry with him for not understanding, but I was forgetting how to feel at all. That was enough for me. He was and is my best friend, and if he couldn't help me I felt no one could. I hardened myself, taught myself to wear the mask and ignore everything going on around me. I sank into my protective shell, one I built myself, not the one built with the help of fellow soldiers, but one constructed out of the self-preservation instinct. From that moment on, I decided I would keep the feelings and horror inside and just not talk about it anymore.

On my first deployment I was able to deal with the horrors of war. Through all the fire fights and all the roadside bombs I leaned on my fellow soldiers and on the training I received at the mobilization site. Whatever happened I knew that we would be able to deal with it. When I finally returned home and greeted my parents I felt the satisfaction of a job well done. I served my country and my fellow soldiers well, and when I was back home, in the arms of my loving family, I could rest.

Because of the interruption in my transformation, on my second deployment, I was not as fortunate. I spent the year of our deployment trying not to feel, shutting down my emotions just so I could function on a day-to-day level. I never made the change from citizen to warrior, because I was one of the unlucky few who witnessed a massacre at the hands of my fellow soldier. I shut down emotionally.

After everything was done, and we were on the plane home, a group of us were joking together and trying to remember the good times of the deployment. This was normal, and I remembered doing this same type of thing on the plane ride home from my first deployment. This time, however, I could not share in their joy no matter how hard I was trying to lose myself in the happiness of my comrades. When the plane landed in Gerald R. Ford International Airport, and we all disembarked, it got quiet in the tunnel going down to where the families were waiting. PFC Robinson was ahead of me, and I saw him speed up as we neared the exit. I could hear people cheering as we walked into the lobby. PFC Robinson grabbed his wife and hugged her, their little boy standing close by, tears streaming down their faces. Looking around, I saw my mom crying. She was holding one hand to her mouth and the other outstretched to me. My dad, looking so proud, face beaming, eyes wide, on the verge of tears, was holding her around her shoulders. My brothers and sisters showed up, too, they were hugging each other and smiling. I was walking into the picture of the model family. My mom grabbed me and threw her arms around me. The rest of my family patted me on the back and started to form a line for hugs. *Well, I guess I am home.* I was back. I survived Ft. Hood. I survived a year in Afghanistan, and now everyone around me was so happy. I felt nothing.

Benjamin Andrus
WRT 150

*Ergo Bibamus*

'Therefore, let us drink'

What makes humanity unique or What makes us human? This is a question that philosophers have tried to answer for thousands of years. While I am not going to try to answer this question myself, I will propose a few possibilities: civilization, religion, art and rule of law. I contend that beer, from the earliest hunter gatherers to modern times, has been the driving force behind not only these aspects but everything that makes humanity what we are.

Ten thousand years ago, humanity was nomadic and scraping together what they could for survival: fruits and nuts, any animal they could hunt and kill, anything that would provide them with the food and drink they needed to live. Sometimes their gathered fruits would rot and ferment into an early version of wine. This beverage may or may not have been viewed as a gift from the gods, but it certainly produced a change or altered mood in the consumers. It was not until humanity discovered grains once sprouted in water and then left to form a gruel that our ancestors knew they could deliberately make a drink that made them feel like a god. Wild yeast in the air would mix with this basic gruel, and the first beer was brewed, causing a dramatic shift in early humans.

What was this dramatic shift in our existence? Civilization. Beer enthusiasts like Charlie Papazian, avid home brewer and nuclear engineer from the University of Virginia, and Michael Jackson, the worlds leading beer journalist, have for a long time believed that, "Beer is the most civilized of drinks. How did civilization begin? With a beer of course" (qtd in Papazian). But is there truth to this assertion? Why did humanity invest so much time and effort into changing their way of life? It was no doubt difficult and possibly frightening for the early humans to abandon their ways for something new. According to Dr. Solomon Katz, a professor of anthropology at the University of Pennsylvania, and Mary Voigt, a research specialist in the Near East Section of The University of Pennsylvania Museum, almost without fail, humans, whether individuals or in communities, will make a huge effort and sometimes even put themselves in dangerous situations to be able to continue consuming a mind altering food or drink (27). According to Katz and Voigt, early human beings, after learning they could domesticate the cereal grains needed for beer production, chose to settle down and collect and grow the wheat and barley because they could sprout and ferment these grains into beer (27). This gave humanity an almost endless supply of this new mind altering food, something they would have been eager to attain. For the early humans, seeking this fix from beer and settling down in one place, where the grains were plentiful and easily domesticated, was beneficial and the natural course.

The benefits of this new brew became almost instantly apparent. As Katz and Voigt explain, "In biological terms, beer drinkers would have had a 'select advantage' in terms of improved health for themselves and ultimately for their offspring" (27). Proving to be more nutritious than wine, this brew became a staple in the early diet of humanity. Beer surpassed everything except animal proteins as a nutritional source (30). The added health benefits to a mind altering brew made this new drink extremely desirable over the ancient wines. This led to a widespread demand for early beer, not only because it made people feel good but it also proved to be good for them, causing the early civilizations to grow into towns and then cities.

Katz and Voigt are not alone; other scientists assert that the driving force behind humanity settling down was beer. "The Desire for drink" Patrick McGovern, the Director of the Bimolecular Archaeology Laboratory for Cuisine, Fermented Beverages and Health at the University of Pennsylvania Museum, says in an article in Smithsonian, "may have prompted the domestication of key crops, which led to permanent human settlements" (qtd in Tucker 6). He goes on to explain the process by which researchers measure the diets of the people of the past and says that the early native Americans, around 6000 BC, were most likely brewing corn or maize before they were eating it (Tucker 6). This fermentation process was not limited to a certain area of the world; while the early Native Americans were settling and fermenting corn, the ancient Sumerians were settling and fermenting barley. Across the globe, beer was helping ancient humankind progress into what we are today.

The settling process was important to humanity becoming who we are, but there were still mysteries to be explained to early humans. Charlie Papazian explains, "Alcohol was not understood. Neither was yeast. But magically these beverages bubbled and made people feel, perhaps, godlike. It is not surprising then that religious significance became attached to these gifts of visions" (6). The widespread availability of beer, which humans could make virtually year round as opposed to the older alcoholic beverages that could be produced only when the fruit was in season, propelled this 'gift' to the forefront of the spiritual mind of stone age humanity.

The sumerians of ancient Mesopotamia even had a goddess dedicated to beer and brewing: Ninkasi. The Hymn to Ninkasi, which includes a beer recipe, is one of the oldest examples of written language (Katz and Voigt 29). Ninkasi is not the only god dedicated to beer and brewing in the ancient pantheons. Michael Homan, a Professor in the Department of Theology at Xavier University of Louisiana, shows us, "In addition to Ninkasi, several other deities were linked to beer and beer production, including Siris, Dumuzi, Enlil, Inanna, Hathor, Menquet, Dionysus and Ceres" (84). Humans have been creating and worshiping deities for thousands of years. This phenomenon started with the earliest settlers celebrating the fermentation of grains into beer. Even today, several of the world's major religions give a special significance to alcoholic beverages. This may stem from ancient beer opening our minds to new possibilities and setting a standard and framework that all religions now follow. It is even speculated that the mind altering effects of beer, on the barbarians that were first settling Europe, may have been the cause behind the spiritual leaders inventing the exotic gods that are depicted in cave drawings (McGovern 21-22). These gods were inspired by the deepest reaches of humanity's mind, and beer gave early humans a way to access these spiritual reaches, thereby creating the first religions in the ancient world.

Humanity now needed a way to depict these gods and share them with others. Beer was the catalyst, which drove the mind of ancient humanity, to develop ways of sharing the gods people saw in their sub-conscience mind. McGovern explains that it "helped foster new symbolic ways of thinking that helped make [humankind] unique" (qtd in Tucker 6). This new symbolic way of thinking possibly even led to a way for us to relive or experience what we see in our dreams during a waking state. The sometimes fanciful images that visit us in our sleep can be vivid, and we can imagine how the first humans would have felt after they were seeing visions in their sleep and could not picture them while awake. Add beer to the equation, and humans can now access those dream recesses of their mind or similar visions while awake allowing them to start representing those visions on cave walls, and art started to take form:

> The stone age murals in their dark caverns thus have strong similarities to dream images that well up in our three-dimensional and often vivid colored fantasies in the dark of night. The deep silence of the grotto, intensified by the effects of [beer], might have nourished the imaginations of sensitive individuals, who then represented their inner and outer worlds in two-dimensional art. (McGovern 21)

Humanity now possessed the tools to take what they saw in dreams and share them with the rest of the community. Beer was drawing the people together and at the same time helping us express our thoughts symbolically or artistically.

Art may arguably be the most human trait. According to Webster's Dictionary, art is defined as "the conscious use of skill and creative imagination especially in the production of aesthetic objects" ("art" 65). With beer providing a strong catalyst for the creative imagination to manifest itself while humans were awake, we can see how it would drive man to start creating art. One of the earliest representations of art is a cave wall in the Dordogne region of France. It is a depiction of a young pregnant woman with long hair who is holding her belly with one hand and a drinking horn with the other (McGovern 16). Humanity was using beer to inspire themselves enough to create and grow various forms of art. It provided the altered state that was necessary for people to create and share these new ideas and was so central to the way ancient humans lived that their first drawings included it.

There are many foods and beverages that provide this same altered state, but for early humans, the very low toxicity of beer made it the ideal source for expanding their minds. Giving our ancestors the ability to develop in ways past cave paintings and pottery, beer caused them to step outside of the box and create higher thought. One way they could do this was with music. McGovern argues, "If emotions and thoughts in early humans... were likely first conveyed by music and other art forms then [beer] can be viewed as nourishing this new symbolic way of life" (McGovern 26). Beer provided an early catalyst for the first artists, and it also helped them to rise above the rest of humankind in expressing themselves symbolically.

One place they were doing this was at Jiahu, in the Yellow River Valley in China. This stone age settlement is the home to the earliest versions of musical instruments, some 9000 years old, (McGovern 32). They were flutes made from the bones of the red crane and two tortoise shells filled with small stones. Archeologists found the instruments in the burial sites of these ancient musicians, along with two clay jugs. The clay jugs were analyzed, and based on the chemical results, contained rice beer (39). McGovern explains that these instruments were used by the shaman of the community. The shamans would use the beer they made from rice and honey to expand their minds enough to create songs and lead their communities in social and religious practices (40). Jiahu shows us how intertwined music and beer were. The leaders of the earliest settlements used beer to be able to create and expand their minds. This form of symbolic thinking is one of the things that give humanity its uniqueness.

In addition to music and paintings, this symbolic thinking may have led to writing. One of the earliest samples of human writing is the Hymn of Ninkasi, a recipe for beer, and a song to worship the goddess of Beer for the Sumerian people (Katz and Voigt 29). Another one of the earliest examples of writing is the Epic of Gilgamesh, and as Homan shows us "According to the Epic of Gilgamesh, beer drinking (along with sex, food and oil rubs) is part of what makes us human" (Homan 85). People developed a need to share the new ideas beer gave them with others. They fulfilled this need by developing a system to convey ideas, not only to people close to them, but with other civilizations nearby. The Jiahu dig site also revealed the earliest written Chinese characters, on the tortoise shells buried with the jugs of beer (McGovern 32). Anywhere across the globe, beer was inspiring the human mind enough to develop abstract symbols used to depict words or phrases, in other words, beer was influential in the development of writing.

With beer bringing humans together and fostering a new symbolic way of thinking, people had to learn to live with so many others in close proximity. One way the leaders of these ancient people handled the convergence of so many people was with the institution of laws. Humanity was struggling through the day-to-day of being a community and with that the first "social traditions have developed that serve to control [beer] by prescribing and proscribing them as a part of ritual practices and social occasions" (Katz and Voigt 27). As Dr. Katz and Voigt assert here, laws or social traditions were developed, not only to govern early humans, but to manage beer and its effects on people. They go on to say that beer was very important to developing the economy of the Sumerians, and that any break in the supply of beer would have been disastrous for them (Katz and Voigt 28). Beer provided a stable economy and a set of regulations for the ancient Sumerian government to build off of and enforce, by becoming an early version of currency. By providing this economic base, from which the Sumerian government could grow, beer became the mechanism of influence, or the tool to control power over the citizens. Any shortage of beer would put the government into an early version of a recession. So then by regulating beer the Sumerian government validated themselves as rulers and provided for their people.

Some of the earliest written code of laws were from the Sumerian and Babylonian cultures. The code of Ur-Nammu circa 2050 BC and the Code of Hammurabi circa 1775BC (Kramer 27). In the Code of Hammurabi rules 108 and 111 out of nearly 300 both deal with the fair price of beer (King). Beer did not stop there, in Germany on April 23, 1516, the German Purity Law, or Reinheitsgebot, was passed. As Karl Eden explains in an article for Zymurgy Magazine, "it is the oldest provision still enforced to protect the consumer" (Eden). There are six different stipulations, all of them applying to the sale and purity of beer. All of them in some way still enforced in Germany today. For example:

> Furthermore, we wish to emphasize that in future in all cities, markets and in the country, the only ingredients used for the brewing of beer must be Barley, Hops and Water. Whosoever knowingly disregards or transgresses upon this ordinance, shall be punished by the Court authorities' confiscating such barrels of beer, without fail (Eden)

This outlines the ingredients that are allowed in German beer. It was adopted to counteract some brewers that were using inferior ingredients causing the beer they made to be harmful or in some cases toxic. Beer provided humanity with some of the first written laws, dating back to the ancient Babylonian and Sumerian cultures. It also gave us the first health and consumer protection laws, the basis of the FDA. Beer made humanity unique by allowing them to create organized governing bodies set up to control the flow of beer to its people and to protect them against dangers.

With humanity now governing itself in a regulated fashion we can see how beer has propelled the human race through time. From bringing humanity together to form the first civilizations, to fostering new and symbolic ways to explain the world through art and religion, to giving humans the tools to self govern, beer will continue to motivate us forward. In modern times beer has given us such technological advances as pasteurization and commercial refrigeration; so it is not so hard to see beer propelling us into the future as it has carried us through the past. Patrick McGovern argues,

> The driving forces in human development from the Paleolithic period to the present have been the uniquely human traits of self-consciousness, innovation, the arts and religion, all of which can be heightened and encouraged by the consumption of [beer], with its profound effects on the human brain. (McGovern 27)

With many anthropologists and archeologists starting to conclude that any uniquely human quality can find its roots in the fermented barley of the stone age, we can start to believe that beer is the reason humanity is what we are today. So the next time someone (over 21, of course) cracks open an ice cold beer they can feel proud that they are participating in a long tradition and uniquely human activity. Raising their glasses high they can toast all of our ancestors and forebears recognizing that what they are drinking is the cause of our unique humanity, and to that I say, Ergo Bibamus!

## Works Cited

"Art." *Merriam Webster's Collegiate Dictionary*. 10th Edition 1995. Print.

Eden, Karl J. Trans. "History of German Brewing." *Zymurgy Magazine*. 16.4 Special 1993. Brewer.org. Web. 26 Oct. 2011.

Homan, Michael. "Beer and Its Drinkers: An Ancient Near Eastern Love Story." *Near Eastern Archeology* 67.2 (2004) 84-95 *JSTOR*. Web. 26 Oct. 2011.

Katz, Solomon H. and Mary M. Voigt. "Bread and Beer: The Early Use of Cereals in the Human Diet." *Expedition*. (1986). 23-34. Upennmuseum,org. Web. 26 Oct. 2011.

King, L. W. Trans. "Hammurabi's Code of Laws." *Exploring Ancient World Cultures*. Evensville University, 1997. Web. 23 Oct. 2011.

Kramer, Samuel Noah. "The Oldest Laws." *Scientific American*. January 1953. *Nature Journals Online*. Web. 27 Oct. 2011.

McGovern, Patrick E. *Uncorking the past*. Berkley and Los Angeles California. The Regents of the University of California, 2009. Print.

Papazian, Charlie. *Joy of Homebrewing*. New York New York: HarperCollins Publishers Inc., 2003. Print.

Tucker, Abigail. "The Beer Archaeologist." *Smithsonian Magazine*. Smithsonian Institution. Aug. 2011. Web. 27 Oct. 2011.

Benjamin Andrus
WRT 150

Traditionally Unprepared

Eighteen years old and just arriving at the university, a nervous young woman watches as her parents drive off after spending a few days attending parent orientations and helping her move into her dorm room. Before this, the longest she had been away from home was a couple of weeks at summer camp; now four years stare her intimidatingly in the face. What life experience does she have to fall back on? What has high school taught her about living on her own, taking charge of her life, not being forced or led around by authority figures? This is based on a typical situation facing most college age children today. Traditional students — students who attend college right after high school — are not prepared to deal with not only the challenging academics of college, but the social changes and responsibilities that college presents to them.

The ACT test is a main way that high schools and colleges determine the readiness of a student to enter college; the three main categories of the test are science, English, and math. The creators of the test developed benchmarks to determine college preparedness in these three areas. ACT Inc. publishes a report every year monitoring the readiness of graduating high school seniors, from 233 four-year universities, for college and carriers, and according to the 2010 report, "These benchmarks represent ACT scores at which students who score as well or better to have a 50% chance of getting a B or a 75%-80% chance of a C or higher" ("Condition"). In the 2003 report they found that 15% of all students that took the ACT did not achieve a benchmark in any of the three categories, and only 28%, of all students in the report, achieved a benchmark in all three categories ("Condition"). In 2010 that number dropped to 24% earning benchmarks in all three categories ("Condition"). In 2003 that means that of all the current college students that participated in the ACT reporting, more than 70% were not prepared by high school to succeed in college. Seven years later that same number jumps to over 75%. The majority of graduating high school students that go on to attend a four-year university are not meeting standardized criteria that shows they can succeed at the college level.

Students that are not academically ready for college will have to take classes they may not want to take, like sub 100 level classes. According to Mike Eichberger, assistant director of admissions at Grand Valley State University, "Not everyone is ready for Math 110 or Writing 150, [sub 100 level classes] are designed to help them be at the level needed to pass" (Eichberger). The idea that not every student is ready for college is echoed in a survey given to professors at Grand Valley State University. One professor explains, "These classes give students, who come to GVSU underprepared, an opportunity to succeed" (qtd in "Survey 1"), acknowledging the fact that students come to college unprepared for the academic challenges. While GVSU offers a way for students to catch up to the college curriculum, high schools should have been preparing these students for higher education. According to Eichberger, those sub 100 level classes "do not count to the 120 credits needed to graduate; they are in addition to [them]" (Eichberger). Incoming freshman should not have to spend their tuition dollars on a course that does not count toward graduation.

The under-preparedness of traditional students for college manifests itself outside of the classroom as well. A study of 1500 freshmen at Queen Mary College, performed by Megan Balduf for the Fairfax County Public Schools, finds that, "From a failure to manage time well to an inability to adjust to independent life, these high-ability students no longer succeeded at their expected level" (287). College level classes require more studying and work to be done outside of the classroom than high school classes, and traditional students have a hard time adjusting to working outside of the classroom, leading to a failure to succeed. One way we see this is in a study of undergraduate business students done by Dr. Sarath Nonis and Dr. Gail Hudson, both professors of Marketing at Arkansas State University. They find, "Having access to a good set of notes while spending time studying only results in higher grades if this time is spent efficiently" (Nonis and Hudson). Students need to learn to manage their time efficiently and effectively to produce good results. Even good note taking skills do not help if the student cannot manage their free time. The study indicates that even if a student spends a large amount of time studying that their cumulative GPA is lower than students who spent a short amount of time studying, but studied with good study habits and were not distracted by noise. Nonis and Hudson also find that "The ability to concentrate always influenced student performance in a positive way...Results suggest that truly studying may not simply be a quantity issue" (Nonis and Hudson). No matter how long or short students study, the ability to discipline themselves and free themselves from distractions like Facebook, loud music, or other social distractions positively affected their grade. Without this skill they end up having too much or too little free time. This free time is filled with social events and other time-wasting activities that ultimately cause a detriment to the students' performance. This is shown in the case of Queen Mary College: "Poor time management led to underachievement: Students who did not know how to handle unstructured time tended to be less academically successful" (Balduf 288). Traditional students need to learn to manage their time away from the guidelines that dictated their high school experience. Unable to do this would, and does, create problems in a university setting.

With students struggling to achieve academic success and attempting to manage their time well, many will make decisions that will negatively affect their lives. An example of this at Grand Valley State University was the Halloween / Homecoming weekend 2011. GVPD reported 23 MIPs that night and "3 probation violations and 4 drug arrests" (Zentmeyer). These come from on-campus violations, and while this number may seem high, the officer interviewed for this article says, "I think the university, as a whole, is slightly calmer, and much of that does have to do with our target Youth Alcohol Enforcement" (Zentmeyer). Because the students lack the maturity to drink responsibly the schools have to react by spending time and resources on a problem that would be eliminated with maturity. This problem is not limited to GVSU; colleges from around the country have the same problem. The first weekend that students returned to the University of Washington officers arrested 97 people (Sudermann). Incoming college students saw the opportunity away from home to experiment and test the limits of what they could do, or get away with. In addition to 33 MIPs during that weekend

> [University Police] also cited three underage drinkers for exhibiting the effects of alcohol and took one person to the hospital for alcohol detoxification. [Saturday] night, Pullman officers followed up on reports of several fights and of people throwing bottles. They also

opened investigations into the thefts of a parking lot sign and a table, both of which disappeared from churches near campus. (Sudermann

This type of activity, while not limited to, is indicative of immature younger students feeling the freedom from parental pressures for the first time. Once free from the rules and constant supervision of living at home, these students make decisions that might leave them with a criminal record or even, in the case of the student brought to the hospital, threaten their lives, because they don't have the maturity level to understand that their actions have consequences.

This poor decision making does not limit itself to the drastic and illegal issues but extends to financial responsibility. According to Sallie Mae's report, "How does America pay for College," a study of 18-24-year-old undergraduates and their parents, the average outstanding balance of college students, on a credit card, is $1,227 with 10% of college students carrying a balance of over $4,000 ("How Students"). What do these numbers mean? According to Capital One's website, the Capital One Student Rewards Card has a 19.8% APR interest rate ("Journey"). That means the student carrying the average balance and making minimum monthly payments, assuming they do not use it again, will be paying on that card for 14 years, and will be charged over $2,200 of interest during that amount of time. Later in that study we find that 75% of students pay nothing on their credit card monthly bill, while only 60% of parents pay on the bill ("How Students"). According to this data there seems to be 15% of student credit cards which receive no payments each month. With this type of discrepancy, we can easily see the amount of debt and financial irresponsibility of the traditional college student. Add to this the cost of college itself. In the state of Michigan, according to a report done by the Institute for College Access & Success, the average graduating senior had $25,675 in student loan debt, 11th highest in the country ("Student Debt"). The average traditional college student does not learn financial responsibility until their credit score is already ruined and they are saddled with tens of thousands of dollars in debt.

One way students have been avoiding this debt, is dropping out of college. Steven Bushong, a writer for *The Chronicle of Higher Education*, says, "In the 2007-8 academic year, 66 percent of first-year college students returned to the same institution for their second year of college, the lowest percentage since 1989" (Bushong). This leaves 33% of traditional first year college students to drop out. Here at Grand Valley the freshman to sophomore retention rate is consistently around 86% (Eichberger). Still leaving about 14% to drop out after their freshman year. With all the information on how college graduates earn so much more money than non-college graduates, the decisions of traditional 18-24 year olds, who are not prepared for college, can have a negative effect on the rest of their lives.

Starting college unprepared in all these ways can lead to disastrous life choices for traditional students. They face a very difficult path through the four year university, while older more mature students are better equipped to handle college. This contrast is shown in a study done by Amy Strage, for the college student journal of San Jose State University. When asked to describe their ideal professor, "Older students more frequently described their 'ideal' professor as someone who was organized...and flexible... traditional age students were more likely to describe the ideal professor as funny...and enthusiastic" (Strage). Later in the survey traditional students described their 'ideal' professor as an easy grader (Strage). Older students are more mature and look for a professor who will help them succeed in college. In contrast, it seems that most traditional college age students are less mature and ready for the challenges of college because it seems they would rather be entertained than educated.

In order for college students to gain the experience and take advantage of the opportunities that are provided them, they need to be prepared to enter the university academically, socially, and responsibly. One way traditional students can prepare is with more strenuous academic preparation for a four year university, such as attending a community college. In a survey given to the students of GVSU they were asked to rank how well prepared they were for college on a scale of 1-5, 5 being perfectly prepared. The average score of students who attended a community college before entering GVSU was 4.1. In contrast, students who entered college direct from high school scored an average of 3 ("Survey 2"). Students who went to a community college before entering a four year university felt they were better prepared for college. This idea that older students do better in college is confirmed with a survey of professors at Grand Valley State University, which suggests that older students are more prepared than traditional students. When asked if traditional students performed better than older students one answer was: "No, I find that non-traditional students typically out perform traditional students usually because they have more worldly experience" (qtd in Survey 1). Older, non-traditional, students have lived outside of the strict parental rules and guidelines that govern their free time. This gives the older students an edge when it comes to managing their time at a four year university. They make the most of the experience there because the time on their own taught them to manage their free time more efficiently than younger less mature students.

The best way to prepare for a four year college degree is not just community college, but to take at least a yearlong break between graduating from high school and entering the university. This option is supported by Harvard College. In an article on their admissions website, William Fitzsimmons, Dean of Admissions and Financial Aid at Harvard College, et al. say, "Harvard College encourages admitted students to defer enrollment for one year to travel, pursue a special project or activity, work, or spend time in another meaningful way...Deferrals for two-year obligatory military service are also granted" (Fitzsimmons, McGrath and Ducey). This time is used by the students to pursue a goal or experience life outside of high school before entering college. For almost forty years, Harvard has been encouraging their students to take a year off. This provides the incoming freshman at Harvard a unique advantage when dealing with the stresses and responsibility of college, possibly one of the reasons they have a 98% overall graduation rate (Fitzsimmons, McGrath and Ducey). This time off, or break between high school and college, proves to be the difference between a successful college career and one that is difficult and strenuous.

How would the opening scene look if the student took time off to mature before starting college? Twenty years old and pulling up in her car to the university, a confident young woman watches as students file into the buildings. Before this, she has spent a couple years working full time and living on her own. This taught her how to be successful in the face of some stressful circumstances. With the economic down turn we are experiencing, she has had to struggle through some financial difficulties, and learned how to manage money wisely. She closes her car door and takes a deep breath, confident that if she could deal with the problems of living on her own, she could deal with the four years of college ahead of her.

Works Cited

Balduf, Megan. "Underachievement Among College Students." *Journal of Advanced Academics* 20.2 (2009): 274-294. *Academic OneFile*. Web. 15 Nov. 2011.

Bushong, Steven. "Freshman Retention Drops, Except at 2-Year Colleges." *The Chronicle of Higher Education* 55.21 (2009). *Academic OneFile*. Web. 15 Nov. 2011.

"Condition of College and Career Readiness 2010." *Act.org*. Act Inc., 2011. Pdf. 22 Nov 2011.

Eichberger, Michael. Personal interview. 22 Nov. 2011.

Fitzsimmons, William. Marlyn McGrath, and Charles Ducey. "Taking Time Off." *Harvard College Office of Admissions*. Harvard College, 2009. Web. 30 Nov. 2011.

"How Students Pay for College." 2011. *SallieMae.com*. Pdf. 14 Nov. 2011.

"Journey, Student Rewards Credit Card." *Capital One Credit Cards*. Capital One, 2011. Web. 16 Nov. 2011.

Nonis, Sarath, and Gail Hudson. "Performance of College Students: Impact of Study Time and Study Habits." *Journal of Education for Business* 85.4 (2010): 229-238. *ABI/INFORM Global, ProQuest*. Web. 16 Nov. 2011.

Strage, Amy. "Traditional And Non-Traditional College Students' Descriptions Of The 'Ideal' Professor And The 'Ideal' Course And Perceived Strengths And Limitations." *College Student Journal* 42.1 (2008): 225-231. *SPORTDiscus with Full Text*. Web. 14 Nov. 2011.

"Student Debt and the class of 2010." *Project on Student Debt*. The Institute for College Access & Success, 3 Nov. 2011. Web. 15 Nov. 2011.

Sudermann, Hannelore. "Campus Party Crackdowns Yield Citations." *Spokesman Review* The Spokesman Review, 27 Aug. 2002: B3. Web. 30 Nov. 2011

"Survey 1 Traditional Vs. Non-traditional." Survey given to GVSU Professors. 29 responses. Grand Valley State University, Allendale, MI. 15 Nov. 2011.

"Survey 2 Traditional Vs. Non-traditional (Student)." Survey given to GVSU students. 35 responses. Grand Valley State University, Allendale, MI. 15 Nov 2011.

Zentmeyer, Anya. "GVPD Doles our 23 MIPs." *Grand Valley Lanthorn* 31 Oct. 2011. 1-2. Print.

Kamara Bailey
WRT 150

## Marbleized

Standing in the kitchen, I battle with the silence that is seeping through the windows from the blackness of night. The cheesecake pan is resting near the warming oven; its glass bottom coated with demolished Oreo cookies and salted butter. The pan's silver-grey sides glisten with oil, bringing attention to the scrapes that have worn through the aluminized steel surface. The gleaming buckle is fastened securely around the circumference of the pan, although the butter and oil will still drip through the base into the oven. The pan is cold to the touch, anticipating the warmth of the oven. It is light to lift; it has only been partially filled. It is late August, and as I grasp the cheesecake pan, I remember.

I woke up to the sound of screaming. It was six a.m.; my summer sleep-in schedule was interrupted as I ran to the door of my room, glimpsing a flash of red hair as my mother hysterically tore down the stairs. I chased her to the basement, where my brother was sitting up in his bed. His eyes locked mine, reflecting the confusion and panic I felt. My eyes traveled to his hand; he was clutching the phone with his index finger pressed to the nine. I could hear my mother mumbling, incoherent except for the repeated word of "no" escaping her lips. I turned to embrace her; she recoiled, crouched and feral on the worn-in evergreen carpet. It was hours before she formed the sentence, "Beth is dead."

My aunt Beth was a diabetic. This was not the type of diabetes caused by consuming too much sugar, but instead was a serious autoimmune condition. With type 1 diabetes, her body attacked the cells that produced insulin, inhibiting her from synthesizing the hormone to keep her blood sugars at a healthy level. She carried an insulin pump attached to her stomach, a device that regularly provided her body with artificial insulin. She monitored her disease with this pump and eating habits but still her body was delicate, susceptible to rapid peaks or plunges of the sugars in her blood. Low blood sugar reactions occurred more frequently than high ones, and left her confused, irritated, and, if not treated, in a coma. Besides her frequent bodily reactions to these uncontrollable blood sugar levels, she functioned quite normally without any other complications.

---

*Kamara wrote her portfolio in the class of Professor Jessalyn Richter.*

She was diagnosed when she was eight; her disease so familiar to me that I never took into consideration how serious it truly was. As a child, I had frequent sleepovers at her home. With a house full of three sons and a husband, she would kick my uncle onto the couch and I would crawl into their big bed for the night. More than once, I awoke in the darkness to her suffering from a reaction next to me. Her fragile body shook the bed, her moans only beginning to build, but within seconds my uncle would rush up the stairs to revive her. On the morning of her death she experienced a reaction like the ones I had witnessed as a child, her body lacking the sugars it needed to sustain her. My uncle had run out of glucagon, a hormone used to raise low blood sugar, and left her with my cousin as he sped out to buy some. When he returned, she was already dead. My aunt experienced low blood sugar reactions often, and so her death was unexpected to all of my family.

My aunt was an artist, able to create masterpieces of all types with her tiny hands. She crafted vibrant glass jewelry and molded clay sculptures, but her specialty was cheesecake. At each of her son's birthdays, they requested a type of cheesecake and she assembled it for them in her timeworn pan. She did the same for Christmas, and I bypassed the turkey in order to snag two pieces of her marbleized chocolate cheesecake. I was fascinated by the simple swirls of cream and chestnut that interwove throughout it, and in my mouth I could separate the colors, savoring them apart and together.

When I discovered that a boyfriend's favorite dessert was cheesecake, I enlisted my aunt's help for his birthday. She arrived at my home, brunette curls piled atop her head, with her weathered cheesecake pan encircled by her ivory arm. She overtook my kitchen, pulling out ingredients from a bag nearly as large as her. She spread the ingredients across the bleach stained countertop, her fingertips bandaged from her many blood sugar tests. Explaining a new method she had learned for shaping glass jewelry, she had not stopped talking since she walked in. As she turned to grab the Hershey bars, she noticed a bowl on the counter I had sculpted in a summer pottery class, and her chattering of her own art switched to fascination with mine. The bowl was horrendous, lumpy and a distasteful shade of salmon, but my aunt was enamored, complimenting me and inspiring me to continue pottery in the future. Although I knew artwork was not my forte as it was hers, I was encouraged. Understanding her as I did, I knew her admiration of me was sincere.

My aunt soon commanded me to chop the chocolate, and I slipped a small piece inside my cheek and then subtly handed her one also. She had become slightly dazed in her excitement over my artwork, and I knew from experience this confusion meant her blood sugar level must have slipped low. I was surprised she did not argue about accepting the chocolate from me. I was expecting her to claim she was fine and did not need a sugar lift. This stubborn independence was a dangerous quality to have in light of her disease, but it also led to some endearing moments. I grinned to myself as I recalled an occurrence when she had nearly been arrested for stealing a Milky Way in the grocery store aisle when her blood sugars dropped too low. She did not intentionally steal the candy bar, but was unable to understand the implications of her actions in her confused state. The store clerks tried to arrest her as she left the store, and though not even five feet tall, she easily convinced them to let her go. She did not elaborate as to how, but I imagined some of her famous swearing must have been involved. For being so small, she was incredibly intimidating when she wanted to be. Her intelligence and determined nature was an easily perceived threat. When I brought this story up with her, her praise of my pottery switched to an outburst about the rudeness of the store workers. I stopped slicing the chocolate, knowing this discussion would take a while.

After taking a breath and noticing we had lost an hour to our conversations, my aunt unwrapped the cream cheese and began to describe her technique of baking as I prodded her for stories of her life. My inquisition about her near arrest for stealing candy must have triggered her opinion about the justice system in general, and her advice for baking shifted to her advice that calling a policeman an "asshole" is probably not the best way to talk your way out of a speeding ticket. Mischievous but not conniving, she sheepishly giggled her defense, "Well he was being an asshole, and when he asked me to repeat what I had said, I told him so." Though this honesty caused her trouble on many occasions such as this, it also characterized her as extremely trustworthy; I do not remember her ever being caught in a lie.

Shifting her advice back to baking, my aunt was in the middle of meticulously explaining how much vanilla to add to the mixture when the ring of her cellphone interrupted us. It was my cousin calling to ensure that her blood sugar level was within normal range. Checking up on her was common between the members of my family, mostly so that we did not find her in a diabetic coma on her living room floor or stealing candy from store aisles. I heard my cousin's voice overemphasize the word "mom" through the speaker, and asked her what this meant when she hung up the phone. Perhaps the best illustration of her unconventional nature, my aunt explained my cousin had been using words like "dude" and "man" around the house, overlooking her because men in their household outnumbered her. She had finally grown weary of this, and turned to him one day, lifted the front of her shirt and exclaimed, "Do I look like a man to you?" My cousin's face turned as crimson as his hair, and my aunt was never called a word remotely masculine again. Shocked by her boldness, I nearly missed the bowl when adding the measured out vanilla.

After spending two hours preparing a cheesecake that was supposed to take only half of one, we finally slipped the pan into the oven. As we waited for the cheesecake to bake, my aunt warned me that cheesecake easily cracks in the oven, and there were certain techniques to ensure the integrity of the creamy center. I brushed off her instructions, and she quickly digressed from the cracking cheesecake into a childhood story of saving my mother from drowning when the ice cracked along their pond one winter. She could barely pull my fur-coat soaked mother out of the frigid water because she was laughing so hard. The laughter from her story relocated to the kitchen, her childlike giggle a staccato rebound off my mother's gleaming wood floors. Imagining my Irish tempered mother's reaction to being immersed in that freezing water longer than necessary, I joined her laughter, our voices contaminating the once spotless kitchen. As our laughter died down, my aunt turned to give me a belated birthday card. It was handmade like all of my birthday cards from her, and scattered with praise filled comments and anecdotes from the conversations we had shared in the last year. Distracted by her inspiring remarks and the memories she recalled that I had forgotten, I barely removed the cheesecake pan from the oven before the cream cheese burned.

The chocolate chunk cheesecake did crack in the oven, its surface fractured down the center. Although we camouflaged this imperfection with raspberries, my aunt called twice after leaving, once at one a.m., convinced we must start all over. Her notorious passion was reflected on the recipe she left me. On the bottom of the sheet there was a small comment scribbled, "Just remember to cover the fucking cracks with anything you can find, strawberries, chocolate, raspberries." With her commitment to helping me, I was surprised she did not show up at my door with another set of ingredients.

I had borrowed the cheesecake pan, promising I would return it to her later. I forgot, and the pan waited, dusty in the dim corner of my pantry. The pan was accustomed to being used, but my aunt did not ask for it back, distracted by her other art endeavors. She died a month later, and I have kept the pan since. I have started to make cheesecakes myself, altering her recipes to create new concoctions. I crack the surface of them every time, and my marbleized swirls never turn out quite right; there are things I did not have time to learn from her.

My aunt filled a room in a way no one else could. Even as a child, I quickly began to realize this fact. When I was eight, my mother and aunt started to test me for diabetes, worried I may have inherited my aunt's disease. I never developed her illness, but I remember wishing I had, somehow thinking it would connect me to my aunt and give us some special quality in common. Though my aunt was expressive, passionate, and slightly outrageous, she never drew attention to herself, at least not purposefully. When she was around, the spotlight did not end by shining on her; instead, she somehow made it shine on me. Though she could fill a room with hours of her own voice, she was entirely content to hear the simplest ideas and stories I had to tell, fascinated by the most mundane aspects of my life. She was authentically interested in who I was and who I could become, and the experience of that pure involvement left me defined, poised, whole.

Though I would not wish my aunt's disease on myself now, the desire for those shared qualities between my aunt and me has not changed since my pre-adolescent years. There was a beauty to the way she moved through life, as though time did not exist. She was consistent in being available for others, never too busy or preoccupied. The baseline for my family, my aunt was the one we all went to when we needed to talk through our struggles. Honest and trustworthy, she did not listen by keeping in mind what her response would be, nor did she act as though she was listening when she was not. She was not known to give advice, besides her comment about the policeman, but instead modeled her unique qualities so well it was impossible not to learn from them. She entertained with her stories and passion, and in the end her combination of involvement in my life and freedom in living left me striving to live as she did. It is through baking cheesecakes that I connect to that feeling of encouragement once again.

I am back in the kitchen. The August heat is causing sweat to drip down the back of my neck, assuring me it is nearly the anniversary of her death. I am trying a new invention, my aunt's original recipe written out in front of me. I can hear her, the comment on the recipe echoing the recognizable trill of her laughter. I fill in the cheesecake pan with my blueberry chocolate mixture; it is heavy as I lift it into the oven.

Kamara Bailey
WRT 150

The Community of Homelessness

I have never heard the words "God bless you" so many times in one day. It is a radiant Sunday afternoon, and I am surrounded by hundreds of pounds of hot dogs, burgers, potato chips, and people distinctly different from me. I am in Grand Rapids, Michigan at the annual Burger Bash in Heartside Park for the homeless living in the city. I am here as part of Grand Valley State University's Hunger and Homelessness student organization that is working in conjunction with two local churches to participate in this event. I am serving hot dogs, and while not as popular as the woman serving burgers, I have gained quite the following. The line to the hot dogs is lengthy, extending across the park, but these people are only a few of the 5,118 homeless individuals inhabiting Grand Rapids and the surrounding areas (Grand Rapids Area Coalition to End Homelessness). These mismatched men and women reach their hands toward me for the hot dogs, some rude, some incredibly humble, but they all thank me regardless.

There is a sense of community associated with those who are homeless in the Heartside area of Grand Rapids. This fact is particularly clear as I observe my surroundings at the Burger Bash. While there are a few families, most of the homeless in Heartside are single men and women, as that is primarily whom the homeless shelters in this area serve (Baker). It is apparent most of these men and women know each other. They shout, converse, and debate as they pass me in the food line. Lounging on the lawn in clusters, they share stories and experiences that I am fully removed from. They seem well adjusted to this wall-less lifestyle, strengthened by one another in their exclusive down ridden circumstances. They are welcoming to outsiders though, and I catch a glimpse of their world as I sit down at a table full of homeless men.

The Heartside community seems better evolved to accepting diversity than the general population. Dave C., a homeless individual who spends his time in the Heartside area, presents this diversity to me as he introduces his friends. Dave points out the redhead first, and through their conversations I find out that he was once an electrical engineer until being diagnosed with epilepsy. Unable to continue his career due to his illness, the redhead eventually found his way to the streets. At the other end of the spectrum is one whom Dave calls his "Indian friend," a Mohegan medicine man with silver braids who was recently released from prison. The Mohegan man carries a weathered backpack full of photos of his handmade dream catchers, and his calming presence makes me wonder what he could have done to merit a prison sentence. Feeling that I am unable to inquire about something so personal, I am left to speculate. While the medicine man is strikingly calm, the variance of these men's behavior reflects the haphazardness of their backgrounds. Some of the men are silent and distant, while others cannot prevent themselves from sharing their stories. Remarkably, their diversity seems to be no obstacle to the bonds they have formed together.

Sporting the smirking face of Bart Simpson across his t-shirt, Dave brings attention back to himself as he reveals his own story. His path to homelessness is one more traditionally cited, stemming from a divorce and a turn to alcohol that caused him to lose his job. In a tobacco-rusted voice, Dave explained, "In 1972, I was owning my own home, making 35,000 [dollars] a year. I used to have it, had it better than most of the people sitting at this table and then some." His past reveals a stark difference from where he is now, having lived on the streets for years, with cracked ribs from being robbed and carrying a deflated sense of self-worth. His friends around him seem to echo this deflated outlook, and they support Dave with incoherent mumblings that give the impression they relate to his regrets.

While nearly everyone is familiar with the issue of homelessness, few people know what it truly entails for individuals like Dave to live without a home. It is easy for those with homes to breezily overlook the possessions they have to navigate through life that men like Dave do not have. As Dave mentioned, "I'm looking for a job, but they all say the same thing, 'we're not hiring, fill out an application, we'll call you.' How are they going to call me, on my shoe phone?" I chuckled at his sarcasm, but his joke reflects one of many issues those without homes face when looking for necessities, such as a job or a home. Lauren Baker, the coordinator for the Housing Assessment Program that is responsible for connecting those in need in Grand Rapids to housing, brought attention to an even more fundamental issue facing those who are homeless. In Baker's words, "All of us have issues of our own, and those of us that have housing take for granted that we have a place we can go back to where we have the stability to then deal with other issues in our lives." As Baker illuminates, we are all faced with problems such as physical, psychological, or relationship difficulties. For those without homes, there is no comfort of a place to process through these problems. With no foundation for stability, it can be extremely difficult for these individuals to tackle the strenuous matters they may be facing.

Although the homeless population is faced with the stressfulness of constant instability, the men I met in Heartside have found a way to adapt to this stress through their relationships with each other. The men in this community share cigarettes, food, alcohol, and places for the storage of their few belongings. While they spend their days walking the city alone looking for jobs, they spend many nights together, swapping bottles of liquor and lighters for a single pack of cigarettes. These might appear stereotypical activities one would expect of those who are homeless, but perhaps not so typical is that these men come together to share their experiences and a place of solidity against a world they no longer find comfort in. Though their gruff voices make them appear slightly rough around the edges, the openhearted atmosphere they provide rivals any close-knit family. The Heartside Ministry, an outreach program designated to help the homeless and poor in the Heartside district, explain their homeless neighbors this way, "…they are brimming with talent, resolute in their faith--hopeful, caring, and deeply committed to the community they have found with one another." This insightful statement explains quite beautifully the men I met in Heartside Park. These men find hope in life in a unique way; rather than trusting that their circumstances will change, they find strength for continuing to be optimistic through the relationships they share with each other.

Furthermore, as Heartside Ministry illustrates, there is a true sense of commitment to the Heartside community for those that dwell there. These individuals are so committed, in fact, that even when the homeless in this community find homes, many of them still spend a significant amount of time in the Heartside area. A friend of Dave's, who comes down to Heartside from his home one hundred miles away explains his commitment this way, "Oh I have a home, and I have money, but these are my people" (Anonymous). This man had once been homeless, but when he found a home, he was unwilling to let go of the friendships he had formed in this homeless neighborhood. His commitment to Heartside is reflected by others; friends who go home at night but spend their days grabbing lunch at the soup kitchens or visiting with their friends in the park who have not made it off the streets. These are not actions performed to take advantage of the handouts given to the homeless; instead, they are ways to connect with the family these individuals have left behind. The individuals who once were homeless have shared a lifestyle with those in Heartside that others cannot relate to, and as a result, they come back to this community to which they are connected.

Although there are numerous homeless individuals fortunate enough to find homes, there are not enough resources to meet the needs of all of the homeless in Grand Rapids. The Housing Assessment Program, in coordination with the Grand Rapids Area Coalition to End Homelessness, is the starting place for assistance for anyone at risk of becoming homeless or who has already become homeless. Unfortunately, this program is unable to find permanent housing for over fifty percent of the households they work with. Many times, there is a waiting list for subsidized housing, or organizations that the Housing Assessment Program works with are unable to provide financial assistance for individuals in need (Baker). These insufficient resources explain why men like Dave live on the streets for years at a time. Though he holds little stock in his overall future, Dave did express to me his desire to find a home for himself. Others in Heartside express this restless desire as well; a balance between exhibiting loyalty to their community while also understanding that homelessness is not a sufficient, long-term way of life. For those in Heartside, they are living in a suspended state, acclimating to a lifestyle because their needs for stable housing cannot be provided for by their city.

While the scope of homelessness in Grand Rapids is already widespread, recently changing laws will cause additional struggles for the homeless community. On October 1st of 2011, a harsher lifetime limit was placed on welfare cash assistance, shrinking the limit from five to four years. Since most poor families use cash assistance to pay rent, it is likely that many more families will fall into homelessness as they reach their forty-eight month limit for assistance (Hoffman). As a result of this law, it appears the homeless Heartside community may be welcoming new members into their family. Though I would expect this community to be hospitable to new members, this influx of homelessness will only stretch the resources that are already too thin.

Though resources are slim, the city of Grand Rapids is responding in a powerful way to their problem of homelessness. The Grand Rapids Area Coalition to End Homelessness has set a goal of eliminating this issue by 2014, enacting policy changes that focus on expanding affordable housing to provide for those without homes. The coalition is also working on prevention-oriented techniques to maintain housing so additional people do not fall into homelessness (Grand Rapids Area Coalition to End Homelessness). This 2014 set date is unlikely to become a reality in a city where the homeless can be seen consistently wandering the downtown streets. However, it does show potential for the future, giving hope to a city that has spent years watching the economy crumble.

On a larger scale, the approach that Grand Rapids is taking to their homelessness issue is being replicated by other cities across the United States. The Grand Rapids Area Coalition to End Homelessness has acquired their method to homelessness from the National Alliance to End Homelessness. The National Alliance is a nonprofit organization that works with federal policy makers, individual cities, and the public to combat and prevent homelessness. Through research, programs, and training, the National Alliance has set forth guidelines to end homelessness that are being used by a combination of 243 cities, counties, and states across the United States (National Alliance to End Homelessness). In this way, Dave and his friends are a small-scale example of a much larger national issue. Though this issue is highly incurable, the National Alliance is using an admirable approach to help both Grand Rapids and other cities battle this debilitating problem.

Though this city and national commitment to ending homelessness is needed to initiate allocation and resource changes for Grand Rapids and beyond, perhaps the most significant way that homelessness can be affected is through a method already in place in communities such as Heartside. Although homelessness may never be eradicated completely, the encouragement that is provided by a community such as Heartside can make homelessness much easier to bear. As Baker states, "We want to encourage individuals, wherever they're at, to build those natural supports and inspire each other." In a difficult economic climate, the Heartside community has formed these natural supports. It seems that, while homelessness is not ending any time soon, this particular community has found a way to adapt and find homes within their relationships rather than in buildings.

## Works Cited

Anonymous. Personal interview. 18 Sept. 2011.

Baker, Lauren. Personal interview. 23 Sept. 2011.

C., Dave. Personal interview. 18 Sept. 2011.

Grand Rapids Area Coalition to End Homelessness. *Roofs to Roots.* GRACEH, n.d. Web. 25 Sept. 2011.

Heartside Ministry. Heartside Ministry. *Heartside Ministry,* 2007. Web. 25 Sept. 2011.

Hoffman, Kathy B. "Mich. Governor Signs 48-Month Welfare Limit." *Yahoo News.* Associated Press, 6 Sept. 2011. Web. 25 Sept. 2011.

National Alliance to End Homelessness. *National Alliance to End Homelessness.* NAEH, 2011. Web. 3 Nov. 2011.

Kamara Bailey
WRT 150

Red-Ribboned Selection

My sister and her husband have been waiting for a child for almost two years, as thirty children die of AIDS each hour ("Report on the Global AIDS Epidemic" 19). Their family is part of a larger trend of families in the United States who are devoted to adopting an HIV positive child. At one time there were mounds of paperwork and to-do notes scattered across their kitchen table, but now it is bare; the work is complete. All that is left in their process is being matched with a child, which could take another six to twelve months. Their adoption process has been occupied by months of fingerprinting, vaccines, child development education training, and both irrelevant and frustrating details. They have been held up by government officials making mistakes on their paperwork, or simply losing their paperwork altogether. Additionally, halfway through their adoption process, Ethiopia, the country they are adopting from, cut 90 percent of their processing of adoptions to ensure quality within their adoption system (Bureau of Consular Affairs, "Alert: Government"). This change has added significant delays to my sister's adoption. However, my sister and her husband are optimistic for the future, and their goal of bringing their Ethiopian child home supersedes the difficulties to achieve it.

Tying herself into the larger trend, my sister explains a portion of their decision to adopt was influenced by information given by other families who have gone through this adoption process (Depp). These families have formed blogs and organizations as they seek to educate about HIV positive adoption and advocate for more families to join them (Project HOPEFUL). This advocating by families is prompted by their learning of the resources they can provide that others cannot, as over half of children infected with the HIV virus die before the age of two without medication (Newell et al. 1236). These families demonstrate how awareness and increasing education are causing the adoptive parents in the United States to both activate and represent the trend of HIV positive adoption. A unique positive cultural phenomenon, this trend is exemplifying how these adoptive families are leading our society to a more welcoming and inclusive standard.

There are no precise statistics on the number of international children being adopted in the United States who are HIV positive, but individual adoption agencies support the idea of an upward trend. Chances by Choice, a program facilitating HIV positive adoptions both domestically and internationally, has placed sixty-five international HIV positive children in homes since its establishment in 2003 (Fleming). Another agency, Adoption Advocates International, cites their numbers of HIV positive adoptions across the years from Ethiopia in particular. Four children were adopted in 2006, twenty-eight in 2008, and thirty-two already placed in homes by October of 2010 (Henderson). Dealing with only individual agencies and countries, these numbers underestimate the impact of this trend. Nonetheless, these numbers do demonstrate the ways in which HIV positive adoption is growing.

There are many reasons why there are no conclusive statistics on HIV positive adoption in the United States. Sara Ruiter, International Services Coordinator for Bethany Christian Services, the largest adoption agency in the nation, stated that Bethany has facilitated approximately a dozen HIV positive adoptions in the last several years. However, Ruiter stated their numbers along with many other agency numbers are only estimates. Ruiter explained it is often not explicitly clear whether a child being adopted is HIV positive. The tests used to diagnose HIV infection in young children are complex and may be unaffordable or unavailable in developing countries. As a result, the verification of HIV infection is not always accurate (De Cock, Bunnell, and Mermin 441; AVERT). Additionally, of the children that are HIV positive, many adoptive parents choose not to disclose this information because of the stigma that still exists against the disease. So although individual adoption agencies may know which families are adopting HIV positive, these statistics are not always widely publicized due to confidentiality for the parents who are adopting (Ruiter). Likewise, the Office of Children's Issues, a part of the U.S. Department of State that handles intercountry adoption, does not keep a record of HIV positive adoptions taking place. Because of these many issues, there is no universal system for tracking these special needs children coming into the United States.

Even without definite statistics on the trend of HIV positive adoption, new programs across the United States are opening to correlate with this trend. In a press release at the beginning of 2011, Bethany Christian Services announced an HIV Adoption toolkit with educational resources to assist prospective HIV positive adopting parents. This agency released the toolkit in response to an upsurge of parents exploring HIV positive adoption (Bethany Christian Services). Another program that is fostering this trend has formed through a collaboration between the University of Chicago Comer Children's Hospital and Project HOPEFUL, a nonprofit HIV positive adoption advocacy group. This partnership has created workshops designed to educate families with medical information about HIV positive adoption to help them decide if they should pursue this type of adoption (Project HOPEFUL). According to Project HOPEFUL, one hundred percent of the inquiring families who have been hesitant about HIV positive adoption before attending these workshops have decided to adopt HIV positive afterwards. These programs illustrate that as families become interested in this type of adoption, agencies are responding with resources to assist and promote this trend.

One of the most instrumental reasons for the rise in HIV positive adoptions is that awareness has changed the way the AIDS epidemic is viewed in our culture. Although there are still many misconceptions about HIV/AIDS, this disease is no longer considered a death sentence restricted to gay men. Instead, it is now understood that HIV can affect anyone, including children born to an HIV infected mother. Although there are many myths about the risks of raising an HIV infected child, this virus is not spread through saliva, kissing, or casual exposure such as sharing dishes (Centers for Disease Control and Prevention, "Basic Information"). While there are theoretical risks associated with sharing objects such as a razor due to the minuscule possibility of direct blood contact, there is little evidence for the fears that HIV can be transmitted through casual interaction (Daar). With improved knowledge of the myths and risks of HIV, parents are more open to the idea of adopting children infected with this virus (Adoption Advocates International, Telephone Interview). Although not eradicated, as the stigma of AIDS lessens through increased knowledge of the disease, children with the HIV virus are becoming progressively accepted in our society.

In coordination with increasing education, another major reason for the trend of adopting HIV positive is that medical resources have changed the outlook for the HIV/AIDS disease. As Linda Walsh, director of the Pediatric and Adolescent HIV Care Team (PAHCT) at the University of Chicago Comer Children's Hospital illuminates, raising a child who is HIV positive is very similar to raising a children not infected. The only differences are that a child with the virus may need to take medication twice a day and see a doctor more frequently than an uninfected child (University of Chicago Adoption Center). As PAHCT clarifies, HIV/AIDS has shifted from a terminal illness to a chronic disease. Due to advances in antiretroviral medications that were not available twenty-five years ago, managing HIV today is much easier and children with this disease can be expected to live longer and healthier lives (Comer Children's Hospital at the University of Chicago). In particular, a study in 2008 found that individuals on combined antiretroviral medications could be expected to live, on average, about two-thirds as long as the average life expectancy for the general population (The Antiretroviral Therapy Cohort Collaboration 297). Although not perfect, these new medications are helping to significantly change the progress of the HIV/AIDS disease. With the ability to confidently raise a child infected by the HIV virus, parents are now stepping forward to take on this challenge.

Another more recent reason for the upward shift in HIV positive adoptions is due to changing immigration laws. In past years, individuals with HIV were barred from entering the United States because the disease was listed as a communicable disease of public health significance (Centers for Disease Control and Prevention, "Final Rule"). Because of this law, those in the process of adopting HIV infected children were required to obtain an immigration waiver, a procedure that increased the adoption process by three to nine months (Project HOPEFUL). In order to change this delay barrier, Project HOPEFUL advocated with government officials and was able to lower this delay to 10 days or less in 2007. Between 2007 and 2010, Project HOPEFUL helped nearly 200 families pursuing adoption of children with HIV bring their children home in a shorter time period. Through Project HOPEFUL's help, the ban on admitting HIV positive individuals was finally lifted in January of 2010 (Project HOPEFUL). Now that this ban is completely lifted, the process for adopting HIV positive children does not differ from children without this disease, and families can pursue adoption of these children without extra bureaucratic difficulties.

Although educational, medical, and legislative advances explain in part the increasing adoption of HIV infected children, there are also more personal reasons why families are choosing these children to adopt. My sister and her husband did not originally plan to adopt an HIV positive child, but were instead motivated to explore adoption because of the devastating earthquake that occurred in Haiti in January of 2010. After discovering they were ineligible to adopt from Haiti, along with most other countries because they are young and have not been married long, they were redirected to adopting from Ethiopia because it was one of the few countries for which they fit the requirements. When the adoption agency brought up HIV positive adoption from Ethiopia, they immediately turned the idea down, afraid of the dangers it might pose for their two young sons. After stumbling across a book about the HIV/AIDS epidemic in Ethiopia and researching the topic heavily, my sister slowly began to change her mind about HIV positive adoption as she realized the fears about passing the virus on through casual contact were overstated. Recognizing the significant need of these children and wanting to adopt a child who would not otherwise survive, my sister's family eventually committed to adopting HIV positive. As my sister explained, "In America we look at people with AIDS and think 'you caused this, so you deserve it.' But when you realized how many children there are that have HIV and have done nothing to deserve it, and also realize you can do something about it, it changes your outlook tremendously" (Depp). As my sister clarifies, both awareness and medical advances changed her outlook on HIV positive adoption. However, most importantly, her family's reason to adopt arose from a deeper desire to help a child in need.

Many other families have personal reasons for adopting HIV infected children as well. Like my sister's family, many individuals pursue adoption without HIV in mind, and the decision to adopt HIV positive comes later as they realize the need for homes for these children (Positively Adopted). Ruiter from Bethany explains that there are also many who cite religious reasons as their motivation. As she describes, "HIV is considered a modern day leprosy by many folks so our families, many of whom are Christian, feel called to help children who many folks just dismiss." In this way, parents are being inspired through their religious beliefs to seek out and take in the children that are stigmatized both in their birth countries and the United States.

Although HIV positive adoption is influenced by compassionate choices by families, an underlying reason that the adoption of these children is rising has to do with decreasing availability of healthy children for adoption. International adoption has been fraught with corruption and abuses of the adoption system in recent years. Countries such as Guatemala have been closed to adoption altogether due to these concerns (Bureau of Consular Affairs, "Alert: Guatemala"). Other countries, like Ethiopia, have responded by significantly reducing the number of adoptions they facilitate (Bureau of Consular Affairs, "Alert: Government"). Because of these problems, there are fewer countries open for adoption, meaning there are a dwindling number of healthy children available for adopting. These issues have caused wait lists of upwards of five years in China and two years in Ethiopia for a healthy child. In contrast, in some cases children with HIV and other special needs, such as those with mental and physical disabilities, are available for adoption right away. This availability may influence the increase in their adoptions (Adoption Advocates International, Telephone Interview). Moreover, for some adoption agencies, there are less stringent guidelines for parents who choose to adopt special needs children. At Adoption Advocates International, single women cannot adopt healthy children from Ethiopia, but they are eligible to adopt HIV positive children ("Ethiopia - Process"). As a result of these regulations and governmental problems, international adoption is increasingly focusing on special needs adoptions. Consequently, the trend of HIV positive adoption is incorporated into a larger shift towards the adoption of children with various special needs.

The more flexible requirements for HIV positive adoption illustrate an intriguing double-sided standard in the adoption industry. By creating differential criteria for these adoptions, adoption agencies are promoting the message that, on some level, unhealthy children are inferior because higher standards for adopting parents are preferred for healthy children. It is clear adoption agencies do not purposefully discriminate against HIV positive adoptions. However, by striving to find homes for these children through lower requirements, these agencies are reinforcing inequality in the way children are viewed and chosen for adopting. In this way, while the trend of HIV positive adoption is clearly visible, this trend is stunted by a stigma that even adoption agencies are unintentionally supporting.

Adoption is not the answer to the problem of HIV positive orphans in our world, but it is a start. On one hand, many of the families who have adopted HIV positive children call it a "Band-Aid" solution (Rachel). Saving a few hundred orphans will not transform the AIDS epidemic, and with long delays for adoption, high costs for adopting, and corruption within agencies and government, adoption is not a possibility for most families. On the other hand, the adoption of HIV positive children is assisting in highlighting a major problem of the AIDS epidemic. Many of these adopting families have come forward in the media through various news sources to tell their stories. By adoptive parents advocating for their HIV infected children, they are bringing attention to an issue that can lead to additional support for HIV positive children and those with AIDS in general.

Although it may seem that HIV positive adoption is only relevant to people interested in adoption or the AIDS epidemic, this trend has implications for all of us. In response to my sister's adoption, I have heard murmured criticisms that we are stealing children away from their culture through international adoption, and that we need to help the children in our own country before helping those elsewhere. However, children infected by the HIV virus are nearly branded to die without permanent care. In an increasingly globalized world, I question why dying in a child's own culture would be more important than living in a foreign one. The lines of our borders are becoming increasingly blurred, and choosing to save a HIV positive child from one's own country over a child from an outside country seems a self-interested, ethnocentric practice. The trend of HIV positive adoption correlates with the larger movement towards globalization and integration. As our world becomes closer, Americans are moving forward to accept the children that other countries will not care for or do not have the resources to care for by themselves.

Awareness, new medications, and the lack of healthy children have encouraged the trend of HIV positive adoption, but it is families with the desire to help who are establishing this movement. As individual families come forward to take on this challenge, they are bringing attention to this issue and prompting others to help as well. Adoption is not an easy feat, and as my sister states, it is only a small solution to a large problem (Depp). Nevertheless, it is a solution that is saving the lives of children across the world that would die without the help of families who are adopting HIV positive.

Works Cited

Adoption Advocates International. "Ethiopia – Process." *Adoption Advocates International.* Adoption Advocates International, 2011. Web. 8 Nov. 2011.

---. Telephone interview. 31 Oct. 2011.

The Antiretroviral Therapy Cohort Collaboration. "Life Expectancy of Individuals on Combination Antiretroviral Therapy in High-Income Countries: A Collaborative Analysis of 14 Cohort Studies." *Lancet* 372.9635 (2008): 293-99. Web. 8. Nov. 2011.

AVERT. "Treatment for Children with HIV & AIDS." *AVERTing HIV and AIDS.* AVERT, 2011. Web. 8 Nov. 2011.

*Bethany Christian Services Provides Essential Resources for Prospective Adoptive Parents.* Grand Rapids: PRNewswire, 1 Feb. 2011. Web. 8 Nov. 2011.

Comer Children's Hospital at the University of Chicago. "Perinatally Infected Teens with HIV Plan for the Future." *Comer Children's Hospital: The University of Chicago.* University of Chicago Medical Center, 2011. Web. 29 Oct. 2011.

Daar, Eric S. "Human Immunodeficiency Virus (HIV/AIDS)." *MedicineNet.com.* MedicineNet Inc., 2011. Web. 8 Nov. 2011.

De Cock, Kevin M., Rebecca Bunnell, and Jonathan Mermin. "Unfinished Business--Expanding HIV Testing in Developing Countries." *The New England Journal of Medicine* 354.5 (2006): 440-42. Web. 29 Nov. 2011.

Depp, Alyson. Personal Interview. 31 Oct. 2011.

Fleming, Margaret. "Re: HIV Positive Adoption Statistics." Message to Kamara Bailey. 27 Oct. 2011. Email.

Henderson, Erin. "We are So Proud of Erin Henderson!"*Adoption Advocates International News.* Adoption Advocates International, 18 Oct. 2010. Web. 31 Oct. 2011.

Newell, Marie-Louise, et al. "Mortality of Infected and Uninfected Infants Born to HIV-Infected Mothers in Africa: A Pooled Analysis." *Lancet* 364.9441 (2004): 1236-43. Web. 20 Nov. 2011.

Positively Adopted. "Susan's Family." *Positively Adopted.* Positively Adopted, 2011. Web. 6 Nov. 2011.

Project HOPEFUL. "About Us." *Project Hopeful.* Project Hopeful, NFP, 2010. Web. 29 Oct. 2011.

"Report on the Global AIDS Epidemic." *UNAIDS Report on the Global AIDS Epidemic 2010.* Joint United Nations Programme on HIV/AIDS, 2010. Web. 30 Oct. 2010.

Ruiter, Sara. "Re: Bethany.org." Message to Kamara Bailey. 28 Oct. 2011. Email.

United States. Dept. of Health and Human Services. Centers for Disease Control and Prevention. "Basic Information about HIV and AIDS." *Centers for Disease Control and Prevention.* CDC, 3 August 2011. Web. 8 Nov. 2011.

---. "Final Rule Removing HIV Infection from U.S. Immigration Screenings." *Centers for Disease Control and Prevention.* CDC, 19 Jan. 2010. Web. 8 Nov. 2011.

United States. U.S. Dept. of State. Bureau of Consular Affairs. "Alert: Government of Ethiopia Plans Major Slow-Down in Adoption Processing." *Intercountry Adoption Bureau of Consular Affairs-U.S. Department of State.* Bureau of Consular Affairs, U.S. Dept. of State, 9 March 2011. Web. 6 Nov. 2011.

---. "Alert: Guatemala Pilot Program." *Intercountry Adoption Bureau of Consular Affairs-U.S. Department of State.* Bureau of Consular Affairs, U.S. Dept. of State, 5 Oct 2010. Web. 8 Nov. 2011.

United States. U.S. Dept. of State. Office of Children's Issues. Telephone Interview. 28 Oct. 2011.

University of Chicago Adoption Center. "Raising a Child with HIV." *University of Chicago Adoption Center.* YouTube, 27 Jan. 2011. Web. 29 Oct. 2011.

Connor Klunder
WRT 150

Helmet Law Hostility

Most motorcycle riders know that hitting the open road on a motorcycle is an experience like nothing else. The experience is often exciting and adventurous, leading to a sense of freedom and independence. Riders are out in the open, in the elements. They can't hide in an interior of a car and aren't confined to an enclosed space. Motorcycles allow riders to experience their environment up close and personal and become one with their surroundings. A wet t-shirt after riding through a rain storm or bug spatters on a rider's jeans exemplify the lack of protection and limitation on motorcyclists. Many riders often speak of the freedom they sense while riding and how good it makes them feel. The absence of protection can actually increase the freedom that a rider experiences because riders don't feel constrained to a certain place or object. In *Easy Rider*, a movie from the '60s that achieved near-cult status, two riders searched for freedom by traveling across America on their motorcycles. They knew the freedom that motorcycling entailed.

As a rider, I have traveled many miles and have experienced that sense of freedom. Actually, I experience it every time I ride and I love it. Riding gives me the power to go and do what I want. But this sense of freedom shouldn't compensate for the lack of safety that motorcycling involves. Riders are so filled with the sense of freedom that they don't realize the amount of vulnerability that comes along with motorcycling. They don't realize it until their first encounter with danger. When I witnessed my brother hit a deer on his motorcycle I abruptly realized that motorcycling is inherently dangerous and protection should never be taken for granted. Motorcycle helmets are a simple form of protection that should always be worn. The mindless task of throwing a helmet on your head could save your life. It doesn't reduce the sense of freedom; it only protects it.

A head or neck injury could kill a person instantly, causing the rider to lose not only his/her freedom, but his/her life. That is why I always wear a helmet, and actually, I legally have to. That's because I live in Michigan where it is a state law to wear a Department of Transportation (DOT) approved helmet while operating a motorcycle. In fact, 19 other states also

*Connor wrote his portfolio in the class of Professor Tamara Lubic.*

have this law, along with 27 other states requiring helmets until a certain age ("Motorcycle and Bicycle"). Unfortunately, the law only covers those 17 years old and younger for most of these 27 states ("Motorcycle and Bicycle"). This leaves only three states in America not requiring helmets at any age: Illinois, Iowa, and New Hampshire ("Motorcycle and Bicycle"). Most Americans realize that motorcycling is very dangerous and should be taken seriously, but there are still 31 states that allow riders to ride without helmets. Despite rights of personal freedom, laws should be in place in every state to make helmet use mandatory for all riders because they keep riders safer in the event of an accident and actually reduce medical and insurance costs for everyone. Having a nationwide helmet law would create safer roadways and better-off communities in America.

Those opposed to the helmet laws say that helmets can actually impair a rider's visibility and hearing ability. James Reichenbach, president of Florida's American Bikers Aimed Toward Education (ABATE) motorcyclist group, argues that helmets are heavy, restrictive, and interfere with riding ability (Galewitz). "Helmets are no guarantee to help you in an accident," he contends (qtd. in Galewitz). Anita Clark, a writer for the *Wisconsin State Journal*, says, "Some motorcyclists say helmets impair their hearing and peripheral vision." Although this argument may seem somewhat reasonable, helmets have been shown to have virtually no effect on hearing ability or visibility. Tim Sass, an economics professor at Florida State University, says, "It has been found that safety helmets reduce peripheral vision by less than 3% and that riders compensate for this reduction by increasing their head movements before lane changes. In addition, helmets do not substantially reduce a driver's hearing beyond that already caused by the noise generated from the cycle's engine." A report from the National Highway Traffic Safety Administration (NHTSA) reinforces this point. It states, "Motorcycle helmets do not restrict the ability of motorcycle riders to hear traffic signals, nor do they restrict visual acuity needed to safely change lanes." Additionally, full face helmets can actually reduce wind noise, making the rider more aware of his/her surroundings. After all, it is important for riders to attentively maneuver on the roadways, as well as hear essential sounds such as emergency sirens. Todd Thoma, M.D., reports, "The University of Southern California conducted 900 on-scene investigations of motorcycle crashes and did not uncover a single case in which a rider could not detect a critical traffic sound." Likewise, as a rider, I know that helmets don't affect visibility or hearing ability and can actually make riding more enjoyable since wind noise is reduced and an added level of safety is present. For me, this actually increases my sense of freedom because I feel safer and more attentive in my surroundings.

In addition, those opposed to helmet laws argue that it is about personal choice and personal freedom. The ability to choose whether or not to wear a helmet gives riders a sense of independence, which persuades many voters to oppose helmet laws. Clark points out that many states, like Wisconsin, don't require riders over 18 to wear helmets, although the DOT strongly recommends them. This fact can be attributed to bikers' appeal and demand for personal freedom. Dave Charlebois, public relations director for the ABATE motorcyclist group of Wisconsin, says, "It's about freedom of choice… I think we all understand that motorcycling is inherently dangerous, but it's a civil liberty issue… as free Americans, it's up to us to decide what we want to do" (qtd. in Clark). While this argument may appear judicious and correct, personal freedom is actually a pretty frail argument. Although freedom to choose may seem like it impacts only the rider, it doesn't. When a motorcyclist is involved in an accident, it impacts many people. Those involved in an accident are put through the American health care system, costing taxpayers money. A writer for USA Today states, "Of 474 motorcycle-accident victims treated during almost four years in Orange County, California…238 wearing helmets had no serious neck injuries…and their hospital bills averaged $16,000, compared to $30,000 for those who crashed without helmets." These costs put a strain on the healthcare system and cost the government more money. As taxpayers, we're all affected. Additionally, motorcycle accidents cost insurance companies money. When riders don't wear helmets and run up their hospital bills to almost twice as much as those who wear helmets, insurance goes up for everyone ("Motorcycle Helmet"). Evidenced by this, the American Automobile Association of Michigan opposes several bills introduced in the House of Representatives that would allow motorcyclists to ride without helmets ("Helmet Law"). Also, riding without a helmet leaves riders more susceptible to brain injuries, sometimes leaving them unable to work for a period of time, or the rest of their lives. California Assemblyman Richard Floyd's office says factors like disability, unemployment payments, and rehabilitation costs contribute to the fact that states with helmet laws have 43% lower societal costs from motorcycle accidents than those without helmet laws ("Motorcycle Helmet"). These costs can drive up taxes thousands every year. So in reality, wearing a helmet is not a personal choice, but a community decision.

Still others say helmets increase spinal injury because the helmet is added weight to the head. Thoma says that "Although in theory this argument would seem to make sense …research has proven this to be untrue. Five studies reviewed by the General Accounting Office all reported a higher incidence of severe neck injuries for unhelmeted riders." An unhelmeted rider's head absorbs the impact of the wreck, whereas a helmet could absorb most of the impact. Evidenced by this, Thoma reports that an Illinois study found that helmets reduce the amount of spinal injuries in an accident. This means that helmets are effective in accidents without causing or worsening spinal injuries.

Additionally, many argue that helmets are only effective at speeds of under 15mph, and most crashes occur at faster speeds. Although it is true that helmets work better at slower speeds, common sense would tell you that hitting an object with your head at any speed would be better with a helmet, and at a point injury would be inevitable. Thoma reinforces this concept saying, "If a rider hits a solid object at high speed with his head, it may be impossible to prevent significant head injury." Still, helmets can only work to a rider's advantage. Those who don't believe this have to ask themselves a serious question: would you rather be hit in the head with an iron pipe while wearing a helmet, or while not wearing a helmet? Clearly, most people would understand that a helmet would protect them considerably more than if they weren't wearing one. Just imagine that type of impact while riding an 800-pound motorcycle on America's roadways. A rider could easily be killed. I know that I would rather have a thick shield covering my head if I were to be involved in an accident, what about you?

Obviously, safety is the main concern for me, as well as many others who support mandatory helmet laws. In order to create a better environment for all Americans, motorcyclists should be required to wear DOT approved helmets. The National Highway Traffic Safety Administration (NHTSA) has stated that motorcycle helmets are 37% effective in preventing death and 65% effective in preventing brain injuries in a crash (qtd.

in Mayrose). Evidenced by this, the NHTSA estimated that helmets saved 1,784 motorcyclists' lives in 2007, and that 800 more would have been saved if they would've been wearing a helmet ("Helmet Law"). Although helmets can't prevent all injuries or fatalities, they are very effective in keeping the rider safer and less likely to suffer from more serious injury or death. As safety is a priority goal for America's streets, motorcycle riders' safety should concern motorcyclists and non-motorcyclists alike.

Motorcycling gives the rider a sense of freedom, but it doesn't give the rider the freedom to be reckless. The decision not to wear helmets while riding affects not only the riders, but also the families and communities that the riders live in. It would be reckless of a rider to let his/her desire to ride without a helmet get in the way of personal safety without regard to the costs it places on his/her surroundings. Motorcycle accidents often result in serious injury or death that could have been avoided by the use of a DOT approved helmet. Many argue against helmet laws, using selfish mentalities and excuses that don't stand up to research and statistics. Mandatory helmet laws should be in place for every state to ensure rider safety and to create better-off communities across the nation.

## Works Cited

Clark, Anita. "Why No Helmet Law for Motorcyclists." *Wisconsin State Journal* 29 June 2007. *LexisNexis.* Web. 5 Nov. 2011.

Galewitz, Phil. "Despite Deaths, No Change Seen in Motorcycle Helmet Law." *Florida Underwriters* 24 Feb. 2006: 10. *LexisNexis.* Web. 6 Nov. 2011.

"Helmet Law Repeal Will Increase Health Care, Auto Insurance Costs." *Science Letter* 16 June 2009: 3576. *General OneFile.* Web. 6 Nov. 2011.

Mayrose, James. "The Effects of a Mandatory Motorcycle Helmet Law on Helmet Use and Injury Patterns Among Motorcyclist Fatalities." *Journal of Safety Research* 39.46 Aug. (2008): 429-32. *ScienceDirect.* Web. 6 Nov. 2011.

"Motorcycle and Bicycle Helmet Use Laws." *Insurance Institute for Highway Safety.* N.p., Nov. 2011. Web. 20 Nov. 2011.

"Motorcycle Helmet Laws Help Protect Everybody." *USA Today.* N.p., 3 Jan. 1992. LexisNexis. Web. 5 Nov. 2011

National Highway Traffic Safety Administration. "Do Motorcycle Helmets Affect Riders' Vision and Hearing?" *Annals of Emergency Medicine* 29.2 Feb. (1997): 282-83. *ScienceDirect.* Web. 21 Nov. 2011.

Sass, Tim R., and Paul R. Zimmerman. "Motorcycle Helmet Laws and Motorcyclist Fatalities." *Journal of Regulatory Economics* 18.3 (2000): 195-215. *SpringerLink.* Web. 6 Nov. 2011.

Thoma, Todd. "Commentary: Advocating for Safety—The Motorcycle Helmet Debate." *Annals of Emergency Medicine* 53.4 Apr. (2009): 501-504. *ScienceDirect.* Web. 6 Nov. 2011.

Connor Klunder
WRT 150

Using Insurance Justly

Some time ago an uncle of mine did something that bothered me. It wasn't anything that detrimental, but it was enough to make me cringe. Actually, I lost a little respect for him after this event. For you see, he always seemed to enjoy life and treat other people well, but this incident was a crime, and that changed everything. It's not like he robbed a bank or anything, but in a way he still stole from a company and possibly even you and I. He committed the serious crime of insurance fraud. It happened a few years ago when he was at his cottage getting his boat out for the first time of the year. He "accidentally" hit his boat trailer while maneuvering his pickup in his driveway. This accident dented up a good-sized portion of his truck, and essentially, he had to get the truck professionally repaired. There didn't seem to be anything wrong with this situation except for two evidential factors: the impact area on the truck was severely rusted, which is an expensive repair that he's wanted fixed for quite some time, and also, the false information he submitted to his auto insurance company. He claimed that a large object fell off a truck on the highway and hit his pickup. The boat trailer wasn't even mentioned! The coincidence of the truck being damaged in the area that was in need of repair was good evidence for insurance fraud, but claiming false information to the insurance company was incriminating evidence. Its people like this that take advantage of the system to get more money or repairs and basically steal hundreds of dollars from innocent people every year. This is never justified, and as a result, it is a crime that is increasingly being detected and punished.

Insurance fraud is beginning to be a real problem all around the world. Richard Derrig, vice president of research for the Insurance Fraud Bureau of Massachusetts, says, "Worldwide interest in insurance fraud, separate from moral hazard, has expanded greatly in the past ten to 20 years." It affects everyone around the globe. The *Sunday Times* in London recently reported that the Association of British Insurers calculated a 10% rise in fraudulent insurance claims in 2010, to an average of £18m every week ("Insurance"). And as reported in *Real Estate and Investment Week*, the Insurance Information Institute concluded that insurance fraud is the second most costly white collar crime in the United States ("HVAC"). Obviously, insurance fraud is on the rise and is not enough is being done to stop it.

The world of insurance is a seemingly excellent system except for the unrealistic assumption that insurance companies can know all the details. Insurance companies have to determine whether a claim is genuine or fraudulent, but it is often hard to distinguish because of the ambiguousness. As a result, many of the smaller cases go untouched and fraudulent claims sneak through the system. And even if the insurance company suspects fraud, it's often cheaper just to pay out on the claim instead of going to court because it is often hard to prove that the claim is fraudulent. Jim Cunningham, a writer for the *Calgary Herald*, said it's hard to prove that something didn't happen or prove that someone isn't injured. The insurance companies can't know all the details and therefore must settle claims in a financially responsible manner. Gwynn Edwards, head of the Calgary office of the Insurance Crime Prevention Bureau, says, "Financially, it's more feasible to settle than to go to court" (qtd. in Cunningham). And this can actually promote insurance fraud. A reporter for *Real Estate & Investment Week* informed, "Many insurance carriers unwittingly promote fraud by paying suspicious claims rather than fighting them." But this is only hurting the insurance industry, and claims that appear fraudulent need to be investigated in order to stop insurance fraud at the causes.

There are numerous reasons why insurance fraud is happening and why it continues to happen time and time again. People either want more money, or just need their costs to be paid, even if someone is paying for it who shouldn't. Tomas Laffey, chairman of Polaris Risk Managers, explains that even dads hurting their backs while playing football with their kids could claim it happened while getting in and out of a truck at work and receive workers' compensation. Most don't have scheming intentions, but just want their costs to be paid. As George Hohmann, a business writer for the *Charleston Daily Mail*, puts it, "Something's bad, an accident makes it worse, and you don't own up to the original condition. There doesn't seem to be much of a consequence." They just want their insurance company to pay all the bills, even though their insurance company was never insuring them for what caused their original condition. This is just what my uncle did with his truck. His insurance company wasn't insuring his truck for rust or door dings, but he got them to pay for it anyway. Derrig states that "[The insured] have opportunities and incentives to take advantage of accidents, even fabricate or cause them to happen, to obtain payments they might otherwise not deserve." In other words, many people know that they can receive more money if they suffer a greater loss. Often people exaggerate injuries or damages in order to make their suffering appear worse. This way they can receive larger payments. Hugh Ross, author of *Settled Out of Court: The Social Process of Insurance Claims Adjustment*, says that "the adjuster typically believes that few people cut false claims from whole cloth, but that nearly everyone exaggerates his loss" (qtd. in Derrig). This reinforces the point that many people use an accident or injury to try to get more money from their insurance company to either cover a preexisting condition, or to just get more money. This is like the people who try more deliberately to get something out of the system, like my uncle. Knowing that the insurance company would cover a claim like his, he went for it and got his truck fixed for free, with the exception of a deductible. Extreme cases of this can lead to a beneficiary of a life insurance policy killing or staging the death of the insured. This would result in the payment of millions of dollars to the beneficiary. The bottom line is that people need or want more money from their insurance companies to cover their financials or even to sustain better lifestyles.

Many people feel like they have a right to take as much money as they can from their insurance company. Policyholders acquire a sense of entitlement, since they've been making monthly payments for long periods of time. Jim Rivait, vice-president for the Insurance Bureau of Canada, says, "It's indicative of this entitlement attitude. People think they have to get something" (qtd. in Toneguzzi). Policyholders want to get the money back that they've been paying to their insurance company for months, plus more. Laffey asks, "Why is it that seemingly honest people think they have a license to steal when an insurance claim presents itself?" There are many possible explanations for this question, but Laffey considers it to be an effect of the insurance industry's attitude. "Could it be that consumers so engaged in insurance fraud do so because almost everyone's experience with insurance companies results in frustration, delay, bad faith and evasive heavy-handed claims practice?...I think this may well be the case" (Laffey). He is trying to say that often many insurance policyholders pay into the system for countless years and when they call upon their insurance company they get frustrated. People sit waiting for money, often less than they need, for a long period of time, or even have their claims denied. This causes them to try and get everything they can out of the insurance company that they've been paying for years. They feel as though they're being taken advantage of and want to get their money back.

Often insurance fraud makes the lives of those committing it better, but it hurts everybody else in the process. Rivait states, "Insurance fraud is seen as a victimless crime and the punishment that goes along with that is pretty minimal…but in the end, everyone who has a policy pays for it" (qtd. in Toneguzzi). In reality, it costs the insurance companies, policyholders, taxpayers, and the government millions of dollars every year. Bruce Fox, an associate at a Massachusetts insurance law firm, says that insurance fraud costs the insurance industry more than $20 billion each year. Mario Toneguzzi, a senior business writer for the *Calgary Herald*, explains that as a result, "Insurance fraud across the country is costing honest policyholders a whopping $1.3 billion a year." And according to Hohmann, insurance fraud costs the average family an extra $1,200 a year. When an insurance company pays out on fraudulent claims, we all have to pay higher premiums in order to reconcile the insurance company's deficit. This doesn't only go for individuals either. Businesses have to pay higher premiums as well. This means that everyone pays more for goods and services (Hohmann). The prices on items on store shelves are a reflection of insurance fraud and how much money it is costing the store and other businesses. Also, the government has to spend money on the court system while trying to punish and prevent this crime. It's a good thing that this crime is being punished, but it still costs the taxpayers a lot of money too.

Insurance fraud should be stopped, but it seems hard to avoid. It seems as though there will always be a way to cheat the system and there will always be people willing to do it. Gary Griffith, inspector general of the Fraud Unit of the state Offices of the Insurance Commissioner, says that the potential for insurance fraud is almost unlimited. "The only limit is your imagination" (qtd. in Hohmann). People can claim anything because it's almost impossible for the insurance company to know all the details. Rick Dubin, vice-president of investigations at the Insurance Bureau of Canada, says it never fails to amaze him how many people think they can get away with unplanned schemes that affect honest policyholders

(Toneguzzi). It's a tough thing to fix, but there are things being done to reduce the amount of fraud that goes through the insurance system. Stijn Viaene and Guido Dedene, professors at the Catholic University of Leuven in Belgium, say fraud-resilient contracts are in place. This means things like deductibles, insurers' commitments to audits through contracts, and imposing legal penalties for fraud. But this still isn't enough. Hohmann states that the fraud unit has evolved over the past few years and has been getting more complex in their investigations. They have even been getting more referrals from their own investigators, insurance companies, law enforcement, other state agencies, and even from consumers. The fraud unit keeps track of past cases and keeps a lot of statistics. They do this in order to analyze past cases and search for future offenses (Hohmann). Also, insurance adjusters routinely investigate claims and negotiate settlements (Derrig). Derrig says, "Companies have the discretion to spend as little as possible (overhead and routine reports only) on a claim or invest in acquiring information (independent medical examinations, accident reconstruction, depositions) to resolve the asymmetry [difference between what actually happened and what information the claimant provides] partially (negotiation) or fully (jury trial)." This costs insurance companies a little money, but it is a worthwhile action to reduce the amount of fraud in the system. Eventually, this would lower costs for consumers, and consequently, cases of insurance fraud would go down because they would be more vulnerable to exposure and prosecution.

Technology has also given a new advantage to investigators. With cameras almost everywhere, it is easy to catch someone faking an injury or even committing arson. Fox points out that, "It [technology] is more accurate and complete, protecting both the interests of the insurer to avoid paying fraudulent claims and the insured/claimant in receiving fair compensation for legitimate claims." Technology can also help with communication. The insurance company can communicate with customers, investigators, prosecutors, and law enforcement faster and more effectively. This avoids critical errors that cause legitimate claims to be denied or fraudulent ones get thrown under the rug (Fox). Technology gives the insurance industry an enhanced sense of security as well as a chance to get more details on specific claims. The reduction or discontinuation of insurance fraud is going to have to be a joint effort between insurance companies, law enforcement, and even you and I.

Overall, insurance fraud is a very serious crime, no matter how small the case may seem. It may look like a quick buck or a good way to live life a little better, but it is a crime and is being taken very seriously within the court systems. Even if customers are upset with their insurance companies, fraudulently making insurance claims is never justified, and in fact, everyone is paying for it right now. It drives insurance prices up for the rest us, including businesses. It's not an action that will go unnoticed. Even though my uncle got away with it, it won't be so easy in the coming years with an increase in investigation, technology, and punishment.

## Works Cited

Cunningham, Jim. "Insurance Fraud Claims Grow." *Calgary Herald* 19 Oct. 1998: B1. *LexisNexis.* Web. 7 Dec. 2011.

Derrig, Richard A. "Insurance Fraud." *Journal of Risk and Insurance* Sept. 2002: 271+. *General OneFile.* Web. 13 Nov. 2011.

Fox, Bruce R. " Technology: The New Weapon in the War on Insurance Fraud." *Defense Counsel Journal,* Apr. 2000. *General OneFile.* Web. 1 Oct. 2011.

Hohmann, George. "Everyone Pays for Insurance Fraud." *Charleston Daily Mail,* 11 July 2011. *LexisNexis.* Web. 1 Oct. 2011.

"HVAC Investigators; Insurance Fraud on the Rise." *Real Estate & Investment Week* 23 July 2011: 39. *LexisNexis.* Web. 8 Dec. 2011.

"Insurance Fraud on the Rise." *The Sunday Times* 31 July 2011 [London] , national ed.: 2. *LexisNexis.* Web. 8 Dec. 2011.

Laffey, Thomas A. "Insurance Fraud: Cause and Effect." *Journal of Commerce,* 26 Jan. 2004. *General OneFile.* Web. 2 Oct. 2011.

Toneguzzi, Mario. "Insurance Fraud Costs Consumers $1.3B: Study." *Calgary Herald* 31 Dec. 2003 [Alberta, Canada] : A6. LexisNexis. Web. 13 Nov. 2011.

Viaene, Stijin, and Guido Dedene. "Insurance Fraud: Issues and Challenges." *Geneva Papers on Risk and Insurance,* Apr. 2004. *Business Source Complete.* Web. 2 Oct. 2011.

Connor Klunder

WRT 150

Learning about Unemployment

Most Americans know that the U.S. economy isn't exactly thriving. Actually, it's in a recession. Cheap foreign labor and production costs have caused the economy to become globalized. As a result, factories are often closed in the U.S. in order to build new ones in other countries. Many companies are trying to reduce costs by cutting jobs and laying off current employees just to compete in the globalized economy. Consumers are frequently hesitant to make large purchases and many feel insecure about their financial situation and their job security. In fact, most Americans know that the unemployment rate is very high. Just how high? About 9.1%, according to the United States Bureau of Labor Statistics ("United States"). Companies aren't willing to take risks. And this doesn't go for just the U.S.; it's all around the world. Unemployment is like a plague that has affected many countries around the globe. Obviously we have to do something to get back on track. We have to accept the fact that we are in an economic recession and deal with it appropriately. But what's appropriate? What can or should be done? Paul Krugman, a well-known economic writer and professor at Princeton University, addresses the unemployment issue in an article entitled "Against Learned Helplessness." In this opinion piece written for the *New York Times*, Krugman emphasizes the fact that much of the world is struggling with unemployment and not enough is being done to fix it. He states, "a consensus has emerged…nothing can or should be done about jobs" (Krugman). In fact, he's even bold enough to say that the topic itself is being ignored. Although I agree with Krugman to a point, I don't think unemployment has a simple fix or a short-term resolution.

As the title of Krugman's piece suggests, people are "learning helplessness." He states "policymakers are sinking into a condition of learned helplessness on the jobs issue: they fail to do anything about the problem, the more they convince themselves there's nothing they can do" (Krugman). In other words, the news of unconcerned politicians causes the people to actually believe that there is nothing else that can be done. Krugman emphasizes that many people have resented making any advancements towards a resolution because politicians and policymakers have laid out a number of excuses and higher priorities before them. Citizens of many countries around the world are learning to be unconcerned with unemployment, because that's what they've seen. Although Krugman makes a valid point with this argument, it is absurd to argue that politicians should offer a quick and easy solution to unemployment. They're not making excuses, as Krugman suggests, they just don't have many solutions to the problem.

One of the excuses that Krugman includes is a recent statement by the Organization for Economic Cooperation and Development, or the O.E.C.D., stating, "The room for macroeconomic policies to address these complex challenges [like unemployment] is largely exhausted" (qtd. in Krugman). In other words, there's nothing that can be done at this point. The O.E.C.D. isn't stating that unemployment can't be fixed: they're saying they've done everything they can do at this point. Although Krugman insists that politicians are making excuses, but he's incorrect in assuming that unemployment has simple fixes that politicians and policymakers can produce. In this case I believe Krugman is guilty of oversimplifying the topic. In order to improve the unemployment rates many things have to occur including working together and not pointing the finger at those in power.

Krugman suggests that even though people in power aren't talking about unemployment, something can still be done. He claims that the core of the problem is debt, mainly mortgage debt, which has created a huge drag on the economy. Krugman says, "Once you realize that overhang of private debt is the problem, you realize there are a number of things that could be done about it." He believes that once policymakers acknowledge this, they'll understand something can be done about unemployment. In a way Krugman is right; private debt may be a real factor in the unemployment issue, but that doesn't mean that we automatically have a number of fixes for it. In fact, private debt is often very hard to reduce or get rid of in a tough economy. A writer for *The Economist* explained, "Nominal growth is essential to bring down the weight of debt. It is hard to ease the debt burden in a stagnant economy with low inflation" ("Leaders"). In order to create growth in an economy, there needs to be jobs. So in reality, we actually need to create more jobs in order to significantly reduce debt.

A resolution Krugman suggests for debt and unemployment is government work programs and mortgage reduction programs. I agree with Krugman to a point; these programs would hopefully create more jobs and reduce debt, but the government has to be able to afford such programs in order for them to be effective. Tom Joyce, a writer for *The Evening Sun*, reports that "Pennsylvania's deputy secretary for unemployment compensation programs said that The Pennsylvania Unemployment Compensation Trust Fund has been tapped out since March. And if the state government can't figure out a way to pay back the federal government and make the fund solvent, taxes are going to start going up on businesses come 2011." This shows that unemployment benefits can often cost states too much money, causing taxes to go up. Nayan Chanda, director of publications at the Yale Center for the Study of Globalization, points out that a legislation was just passed extending unemployment benefits up to 99 weeks. This could increase government debt and harm the growth of the economy, and possibly damage the job market. Nonetheless, The U.S. department of Labor already has sponsored work programs to help the unemployed get back to work and sustain an income.

Krugman overlooks the fact that policymakers and politicians have considered all the factors of unemployment, including debt, when brainstorming resolutions to unemployment. Chanda says, "In the current deficit battle, the US focuses on reducing the debt burden and not on job creation as the ultimate path to financial health." In effect, the U.S. government has been more fixated on debt lately than on unemployment. It's not as if everyone is ignoring debt and debt-reducing programs as Krugman suggests. I agree with Krugman that debt reducing programs could help unemployment, but we can't rely on them to reduce unemployment extensively. An article in *The Economist* states that although debt reduction works, it is going to take even the richest economies years to perform ("Leaders"). Therefore, debt reduction is not a quick and easy resolution to unemployment. Although Krugman is accurate in distinguishing a connection between debt and unemployment, he's incorrect to make the conclusion that reducing debt is going to solve the unemployment problem.

Another reason for the lack of response to unemployment that Krugman mentions is the Republican Party. He states "who is talking seriously about job creation these days? Not the Republican Party... any effort to tackle unemployment will run into a stone wall of Republican opposition." Krugman is correct in the fact that the Republicans have opposed unemployment policies such as the extension to unemployment benefits. Annie

Lowrey, an economic and business writer for *Slate Magazine*, says that Republicans argue that the extension isn't paid for. Approving this policy would create a deficit in the nation's funds, creating more debt and less opportunity for employment. Krugman would argue that giving the unemployed more money would encourage spending and would stimulate the economy, but in reality, the unemployed would probably save as much of the money as they could because they need it for future bills and expenses.

Paul Krugman is accurate in saying that unemployment is high around the world and that we are in need of some kind of improvement. But Krugman is distinctly wrong to announce that the topic is being ignored and nothing is being done to fix the problem. Krugman is even audacious enough to point the finger at the people in government, and more specifically, the Republican Party. In reality, the high unemployment rates aren't the responsibility of a single group or political party, but the entire globalized economy. I think Krugman has undermined the size of the issue at large. Unemployment certainly doesn't have a simple resolution like a program or policy and cannot be fixed only by a particular group of people. Renovating the unemployment issue is going to have to be a joint effort by everyone around the world. For certain countries it may require raising or lowering taxes, for others it may not. For some countries it may require government sponsored programs, and others it may not. Unemployment won't be a simple fix for every country, but with time and everyone's effort we can stimulate the economy, create jobs, reduce debt, and reduce high unemployment rates.

Works Cited

Chanda, Nayan. "Employment Versus Debt." *YaleGlobal Online*. N.p., 26 July 2011. Web. 17 Sept. 2011.

Joyce, Tom. "State's Unemployment Fund Tapped Out." *The Evening Sun*. N.p., 26 Jan. 2010. *LexisNexis*. Web. 23 Oct. 2011.

Krugman, Paul. "Against Learned Helplessness." *The New York Times*. N.p., 29 May 2011. Web. 13 Sept. 2011.

"Leaders: Handle with Care; Debt reduction." *The Economist*. N.p., 9 June 2011. *ProQuest*. Web. 22 Oct. 2011.

Lowrey, Annie. "Clueless About the Jobless." *Slate*. Washington Post Company, 1 Dec. 2010. Web. 17 Sept. 2011.

"United States Unemployment Rate." *Trading Economics*. N.p., 2011. Web. 13 Sept. 2011.

Claire Norman
WRT 150

## Gymnastics' SUPER TwiSTARS

She is an ordinary sixteen year old girl with an extraordinary talent; he is
a typical work-oriented individual with a not-so-typical job. She is qui-
etly composed, yet fiercely powerful; he is wildly ambitious, but precisely
organized. She is Jordyn Wieber, he is John Geddert, and together they are
World Champions.

Jordyn Wieber began gymnastics in 1999 at the early age of four. Only
twelve years later she is the best gymnast in the world and has a title to
prove it. On October 13, 2011 Jordyn captured the gold medal at the
World Gymnastics Championships in Tokyo, becoming only the sixth
American in history to hold this title. As Jordyn competed for the title
in Japan, teammates back home huddled together at 5:00am on the gym
floor. They were determined to be there in spirit as their teammate took on
the biggest competition of her life. Stacked high on gymnastics mats, they
had connected their computer to a television so they could view the live
online stream of the Championships. It was an intense battle for the gold,
and they could feel the pressure as Jordyn fought for every tenth of a point.
When the final results flashed, they saw her face flood with emotion as
she tearfully embraced long-time coach, John Geddert. "Two dreams were
realized at that moment; Jordyn's dream of being a world champion and
my dream of coaching one" Geddert later blogged in his online journal.
Training at the same gym for your entire career is quite rare in the world of
gymnastics, but Jordyn and John have stuck together. Their relentless hard
work and perseverance over the years have paid off. This vibrant, dynamic
duo has respectfully worked their way into gymnastics royalty.

The gold medal from Tokyo would find its new home halfway around
the world in Dimondale, Michigan. In 1996 John and Kathryn Geddert
started Twistars Gymnastics Club USA at The Summit in Dimondale. A
few years later, four year old Jordyn Wieber joined the husband-wife duo
at the 15,000 square foot gymnastics facility. Jordyn took to the sport
immediately and was in level 5 (usually recognized as the first competitive
level) by age seven. With the help of the Gedderts, she progressed through
the levels winning various medals and awards. At the innocent age of ten

*Claire wrote her portfolio in the class of Professor Michele Lussky.*

Jordyn was performing gymnastics skills equivalent to those of the nation's most prominent college recruits. By 2006 she was competing as a level 10, the highest level in the Junior Olympic (J.O.) Program. She took no time establishing a name for herself, finishing 2nd at the J.O. National Championships during her first year as a level 10. In mid-2006 Jordyn qualified as an elite gymnast and received her first international assignment: the 2006 U.S. Classic in Kansas City. Next were the Visa Championships in which she placed 9th in the All-Around, earning her first chance to represent the United States on the elite National Team at the mere age of eleven.

The next five years Jordyn flipped her way through the elite program capturing numerous titles, her coach by her side every step of the way. In 2007 they brought three gold medals, one bronze medal, and one silver medal home from Guatemala. 2008 meant both team and individual all-around gold in Italy as well as Belgium, a clean sweep of five gold medals in Houston, and the notable title of United States Junior National Champion. 2009 followed on strong with gold at the American cup and five more in Canada. This year started with a solid win at the Visa Championships and finished with her most prized title as World Champion. She also helped the U.S. team, with Geddert appointed as their head coach, to the team gold at the World Championship. Wieber Fever, a term fans have coined, has undoubtedly become an epidemic. So what is next? Jordyn is a favorite for next year's gold at the 2012 Olympic Games in London, but for now she keeps a focus on everyday practice in the gym and her junior year of high school.

She may be soaring through the air on your television screen, but back in Dimondale Jordyn is your simple teenage girl. While many elite gymnasts sacrifice public schooling due to a demanding training schedule, Jordyn has managed to coordinate a schedule that allows for school and gymnastics. She admits "It would probably be easier to just do home schooling, but going to school keeps things normal…and I like seeing friends" (Wieber). Some weekdays involve morning and evening training, so she must do online classes in addition to her attendance at DeWitt High School. It seems that, at sixteen, she has better time management skills than most adults. She even finds time for leisure activities; shopping and fashion are among her favorites, along with trips to the movies and time with friends. All of this would not be possible without some help from Geddert, who makes productivity a priority at practice.

Geddert has set up a training schedule that requires just over 30 hours a week in the gym. This is on the low end of the scale, as many elites train 35-40 hours a week or more. While Geddert knows that training for the Olympics requires maximum attention, he understands that too many hours in the gym can lead to physical and motivational issues. There is no perfect training model for coaches to follow, so he must go with his knowledge and experience in creating a schedule that will be the most beneficial to his athletes. It's a fair assumption that his program must be working, given that Twistars has produced over 40 national champions. Although Geddert has a detailed systematic approach to coaching, smiles and laughs are always welcome at practice. His philosophy is to "Keep a positive environment where the girls can have fun and feel good about their gymnastics" (Geddert). This philosophy is not just a mission statement that John writes in his handbook; after my visit to Twistars it became clear that he emanates every aspect of it in his daily work.

* * *

I walk into the Summit at Capitol Centre in Diamondale, a multi-sport facility, and head toward the Twistars banner that hangs above the entrance to the gymnastics center. Underneath the banner is a table that proudly displays plaques, pictures, and a blown up article from the *Detroit Free Press* highlighting Jordyn and John's recent accomplishments at the World Championships. I browse through the material for a minute and then make my way through the doors into the gym: the place where it all began.

It is a Friday night in early November, but the lighthearted smiles from Twistars gymnasts filtering through the doors indicate no concern over giving up various school football games for practice. It is hard not to instantly notice Jordyn, with her chiseled frame and refined movements. Her body is perfectly sculpted for a gymnast; her muscles are tightly toned, but she maintains the graceful physique of a young woman. She gathers together with the other girls on the floor as they share stories about their day and the latest news. They do a few stretches on their own and then begin the group warm up. While they jog, leap, and jump around the floor each gymnast seems to be mentally preparing for a positive workout. Kathryn Geddert stands on the sidelines making sure the girls are taking their warm-up seriously and preparing their bodies for the night's practice. "Get a move on it" she urges as she makes a quick get-going gesture with her arm. The team looks like a well-oiled machine as they go through their synchronized warm-up movements, but they all seem to have smiles and are not silenced from talking and laughing with one another. Kathryn throws in a few more corrections and after about twenty minutes of fast paced exercises they slow down for some flexibility. Jordyn may be a powerhouse, but flexibility does not come easy and I notice her eyes in a deep focus as she pushes her legs and shoulders to their full extent. Her callused hands reach up to secure her ponytail as she readies herself for the workout ahead.

Jordyn lines up with the other girls as they are broken into smaller groups and assigned to their first event. She chats and walks with her group toward the balance beams. As I watch and listen I begin to realize that inside these gym walls she is just Jo; a compassionate teammate that focused on her dreams and happened to become World Champion along the way. Then I look over at John and Kathryn Geddert as they get ready for the first rotation of coaching. Kathryn has her arms around one of the gymnasts and John is headed toward me. He courteously tells me to make myself at home and cracks a joke after I trip over a mat. It is clear that I have been welcomed with open arms. Only thirty minutes into my visit and I now know that this Twistars team is a family and this gym is their home.

The girls all hop up onto their own high beam. Four feet above the ground they begin their beam complex: a series of walks, hops, scales, and positions to get them ready for the more difficult elements. They seem to have the complex memorized and do not need much direction or correcting from their coach in completing it. Each girl then has her own daily assignment to complete in an hour. Now the true gymnast in them comes out. Jo automatically whips out some of the most difficult skills in the sport of gymnastics, including a standing back flip with a full twist in the air connected to an immediate back handspring. You might expect some hesitation or fear as she is flipping and twisting on a four-inch wide apparatus high above the ground, but this girl is attentive and aggressive. She stops for a second to fix the bandage on her leg, and laughingly says to Kathryn "This blood is like gushing everywhere, it won't stop coming out" (Wieber). It must not be anything too serious, as she hops back up on the beam within seconds. Jo continues through her assignments, keeping a count by making little marks with her nail on the end of the balance beam each time she executes a skill perfectly. A teammate interrupts to ask Jo if she has seen *Paranormal Activity 3* at the theatre yet. She quickly replies and gives her input on the movie, but removes herself from the ongoing conversation after a minute so she can get back to business. The gymnasts work through their assignments, do some drills, and talk or rest here and there. Jo is in a different world though. As I watch it seems like she is in a zone of perfection. The rest of the gym keeps spinning around her, but Jo is in total control and focus while she is up on the beam. She is always mindful of her surroundings, but keeps a profound concentration on the task at hand. As Jo wraps up her beam workout and the hour comes to an end, the group moves on to the uneven parallel bars.

Bars begin with each gymnast putting on their hand grips, which help reduce friction and allow for better grasping of the bar. This is when John comes into play, as his wife stays behind to help the next group on beam. John is a gymnastics encyclopedia. He is the most decorated women's gymnastics coach in Michigan history and has produced well over 40 National Champions at the Junior Olympic and Elite levels. Surprisingly his 30 plus years of experience are not what have me in awe as I watch John at work with the gymnasts. Instead, it is his captivating charisma and motivational magnetism that have me at a loss for words. Everything about him screams hard work, detail, and success. Jo adjusts some athletic tape around her thumbs, sprays her grips with water, applies chalk, and jumps to a front support on the bar. It's hard to ignore the obvious coach-athlete chemistry between Jordyn and John on the bars. There is no dialogue necessary between the two; he can tell from her body language when he will need to step in and spot her. Instead, the dialogue comes when Jordyn surprises Geddert by completing a Weiler out of her Shapashnikova half (he had expected just one of the two moves). As she muscles out the two tricks, he proudly smiles "Wooohoohoo...now she's on a roll!" (Geddert). Jo's response is different: she smiles at his approval, but was hoping to add yet another Weiler to the combination. This is the perfectionism that has earned her the top title in the gymnastics world. The chalk dust settles and I am taken back by the amazement of the atmosphere. There is a certain aura that radiates as John and Jo work; a positive vibe that lets you know you are in the presence of greatness. After an hour on bars, John looks at me to see what I thought of their bar workout. I just smile, nod my head in amazement, and make my way toward the floor exercise.

Next up is floor dance, where Jo will lead off her group. She positions herself in the corner of the floor, her arms crossed in front of her and her leg extended backward in her beginning pose. As "Wild Dances" begins to play Jo expressively lights up the floor. The music, a selection from *Cirque Du Soleil* by Ruslana, is full of sassy, energetic beets and a few vocals. It is a perfect match for Jo and she showcases her captivating personality as she performs her routine. The intense focus is still there, but you can see the spark of a champion in her presentation and smile. When her routine is done, she takes time to help one of her teammates on a dance element. She might be training for the Olympic Games, but she's not too busy to share her gift and help a friend improve.

The camaraderie of the girls shows even more as they move on to conditioning. They partner up for some strength training and push each other toward perfection. The strength training is pretty intense, but the girls talk each other through the exercises with mental toughness. As they move on to floor tumbling, it is clear that there is no jealousy among the Twistars family. They cheer each other on and seem to share every emotion of struggle or accomplishment with one another. There is a positive respect among this family of gymnasts and coaches that distinctly explains their success. In two lines they pound out tumbling passes one after another, sometimes even amazing themselves. "Jooohnn, can you get me?" Jo yells from the end of the floor before her double twisting double back (Wieber). The pass looks polished, but John is there for security and comfort. After a couple more she signals him to move away and does one on her own, exploding into the air and nailing the landing with exact precision. Jo looks over to John for his critique, "Not bad for a girl" he mocks with satisfaction (Geddert).

After hammering out a few vaults, practice concludes with some calm and focused stretching. The Twistars share some hugs, laughs, and talk a little before heading home. John "Doesn't like the thought of her behind the wheel on her own", but Jo recently got her license and will make the twenty minute drive home to DeWitt (Geddert). She will be back at the gym tomorrow, but for now she heads to her actual home and family.

The Wiebers are a family of athletes, but there is no denying that Jordyn is in a league all her own. This is not to say she is exempt from pulling her weight at home however. Even the World Champion is expected to keep her room clean and do her own laundry. The Wiebers are a close-knit family and find time between their demanding schedules to support one another. Jordyn loves visiting her older sister who lives a couple hours away, cheers from the stands when her quarterback brother has a football game, and helps drive her younger sister around when mom and dad are busy. They attend church together on Sundays; something that Jordyn says is important to her and helps her stay grounded.

When asked if she has a favorite motivational quote, Jordyn responds "Well, one I think about a lot is the Bible verse 'I can do all things through Christ who strengthens me' (*New King James Version*, Philippians 4:13)". She may only be a teenager, but her age is no indication to the depth of her abilities. As I drive home from The Summit, my mind tumbles through all the excitement of my experience and it is certain that I have caught the Wieber Fever.

Only time will tell what is in store for Jordyn and John, but I have a feeling this is only the beginning of their success. As they continue in an effort to make their next dream a reality, I am left with the idea that "You are only as good as your next performance" (Geddert). There is some rare magic going on in Dimondale, Michigan and the future looks bright for these Twi*stars*.

## Works Cited

Geddert, John. Personal interview. 4 Nov. 2011.

Wieber, Jordyn. Personal interview. 4 Nov. 2011.

Claire Norman
WRT 150

Riding like a Girl

My grandpa, Joe, got the call around 7:30pm on December 4, 1986. His first daughter had just given birth to an 8.6 pound baby girl and her name would be Claire Elizabeth. Mom and baby were healthy and could not wait to come home. As he hung up the phone, Joe smiled from ear to ear. He had stayed back home to watch Michael, his daughter's first child, who was four years old and too young to be romping around the hospital. The two of them had been anxiously awaiting this phone call for hours; Joe praying for his daughter to give birth to a healthy grandchild and Michael praying with all his might that he would have a new baby brother. Michael looked up at his grandpa, "Did mom have the baby?" he asked in desperate anticipation. "You betcha, you have a new baby sister" Joe replied. Michael's face was instantly struck with disappointment as he stomped his foot, ran to his bedroom, and barricaded the door shut. When my mom got on the phone at the hospital all she could do was laugh; my grandpa had called asking what to do with Michael's Fort Knox response to her having a girl instead of a boy. "He is four years old, figure it out dad!" she joked.

I have probably been told that story a hundred times; the story about how unexcited my brother was that I had turned out to be a girl. I was obviously not there to experience his tantrum, but knowing my brother, I can only imagine what my poor grandpa had to deal with. Michael has always had the stubborn rottenness of that trick candle on your birthday cake; it is going to stay lit whether you like it or not. When he has his mind set the world had better stop and attend to him, otherwise he might just lock himself in the bedroom and not come out! He must have something good about him though, because for a while all I wanted to do was be just like Mike.

After a few years I was following my brother everywhere I could. As soon as he would get home from school I would be like a barnacle on a whale. Mike was about as active and wild as they come, so we spent most of our time outdoors. He could climb the tallest trees in the park, hit any baseball you pitched at him, and win wrestling matches with kids twice his size. Somehow he had even braved getting stitches in his mouth after

biting his tongue in half during a game of dare. I would try to do everything the way he did, but somehow he always did it better. He loved that
of course, and never made it easy on me. If I scraped my knee trying to
climb as high as he did in the tree, he would laugh and tell me I needed
better footing. When I wanted to learn to play baseball like him, he gave
me a mitt and whipped the ball at full speed toward my face. Wrestling was
a joke, because before I could try one move he would have me flat on my
back, shoulders down yelling "Pinned ya!" with a merciless grin. I climbed
and wrestled my days away hoping that maybe, just maybe, I could do
something as good as my brother. If I could master just one thing to show
him how tough I was, maybe then he would teach me all his other stunts. I
don't know if it was his ego or if he was still determined on me being a boy,
but he made this close to impossible. I suppose that is why this particular
day seems vividly etched in my mind twenty years later.

It was a breezy spring day shortly after my fifth birthday. After school
Mike went straight to our shed in the backyard, and I of course followed.
The first thing he grabbed was his toolbox, which was never a good sign.
The next thing he had his eyes set on was my bicycle. He carefully pulled it
out of the shed and wheeled it into the grass. He stared at it for a minute
and I could just tell he was spinning ideas in that head of his. I thought for
sure he was going to take the whole thing apart, piece by piece. He had a
bit of a reputation for dismantling things around the house and then attempting to put them back together; mom was never too fond of this since
he often struggled with putting them back together. I may have been worried that my bike was doomed for disaster, but I kept my mouth shut in
fear of him dismantling me instead. He crouched down and slowly began
his task. Much to my dismay, the first thing he went for were the trusty
training wheels. He had those off in no time and reached back for his
toolbox. I could barely look as I imagined what would be next, probably
the streamers I had gotten for my birthday. He fumbled his hand through
the toolbox and pulled out some kind of cloth. He began to rub down my
bike, top to bottom. This had me confused and I finally mustered up the
courage to intervene. Ever so quiet and innocent I uttered "Um..Mike…
uh…why do you have to polish it before you take the rest of it apart?" He
turned and looked at me with a grin. That was it, I had done it. I should
have just let him go and minded my own business. He took a step back

from the bike and facing me, gently laid both his hands on my shoulders. He must have felt me quivering in fear and began to respond "Claire, I'm done taking it apart. It needs to be nice and shiny for you when I teach you how to ride without the training wheels."

Something about the way he looked at me when he said it, with a gracious and faithful glimmer in his eye, had me stunned. My stubborn-rotten, bossy brat of a brother was going to teach me how to ride without training wheels? I am not sure what subject his teachers went over in school that day, but it must have been a good one. Mike was finally going to teach me one of his tricks, and from the sound of it he was going to be helpful instead of horrible. After a minute of shock I looked over at my bike. For some reason it looked better than it did the day I got it.

It was a light powder blue like the sky on a calm summer day. The streamers were new and ruffled in the breeze as if they were waves in the ocean. The sparkles and turquoise horn added that extra bit of character. The reflection from the sun on the silver handlebar made it seem like it was embellished with diamonds. It stood there, proudly displaying its new freedom from training wheels, and begged me to take it for a ride.

Mike went in the house to tell my mom that we were headed across the street and told me to meet him in the front yard with my bike. There was a doctor's office across the street with a big parking lot that was usually pretty empty. When we got the bike over there Mike explained to me how things were going to work. "Alright Claire, I'm going to hold it steady while you get on. I'll keep holding it and walk next to you as you pedal. I promise I won't let you fall. We'll just keep trying until you get it, you'll be fine" he clarified as he gestured me on to the seat. Then we started, slowly at first because although I was eager, I was still a little girl terrified of two wheels. I cautiously turned the pedals over one by one, by one, by one. He walked and I pedaled for what seemed like days. Mike held his promise though as he walked along side me patiently persuading me to pick up a little speed. Eventually I began to trust him and found myself pushing at the pedals harder and harder, my brother now jogging at my side. Every positive attempt with reassurance from Mike added to my confidence and determination. I was a rookie soldier preparing for battle, with the best Master Sergeant mentoring me along the way. He never told me I had to do it on my own; instead he waited for me to give him the signal that I was ready.

"Okay Mike, I think I want to try it this time. When I get going steady then you can let go, but make sure I'm really balanced" I told him.

My hands were gripped perfectly around the handlebars and I sat straight up on the seat. As I prepared for take-off my eyes were focused straight ahead, my lips pressed tightly together, and both feet strategically placed on the pedals. I was perfectly poised and postured, ready to take on any treacherous pothole or rock that got in my way. As we took motion I could feel the power building inside me. I pedaled and pedaled and then it happened; my brother's hands lifted off my bike and faded away. I kept focused on the task and hand and rode straight across the entire parking lot, just me and my two white wheels. I pressed on the brakes and put my feet down. Swinging my leg over the seat I turned to look at my brother who was running toward me. He gave me a big hug, scooped me up, and told me how proud he was of me. In my mind I had won the World Series. I was still a girl, but I was a girl who could ride a bike right alongside her brother.

That summer I rode my bike everywhere. Mike and I would ride our bikes around the school, bike with mom down to the grocery store, and even ride around on the grass in our backyard. Riding my bike was fun, but I learned something that would make me even happier that day. I learned that the stubborn-rotten boy that shut himself in his room years ago had fallen in love with his little sister.

Claire Norman
WRT 150

Man and the Missile

Although I am a native of Michigan, four of my last five years were spent living in Great Falls, Montana with my husband. While Montana is home to undeniable breathtaking scenery, our experience there consisted of a rather different focus. We made the move out west when my husband, Josh, was given orders to Malmstrom Air Force Base (AFB) by the United States Air Force. In a matter of months his assignment to Montana unfolded details that would make a drastic impact on both of our lives; we quickly learned that Malmstrom is home to the 341st Space Wing and its main mission centers around our country's nuclear missiles. Josh's duty as a Security Forces Officer would be to protect these missiles. To say the least, securing our nation's nuclear missiles is a job that requires a rather strict schedule and way of life. With my husband playing such a critical role in our nation's security, I became more interested in global news and foreign policy. I knew that every issue could have a direct impact on Josh's job and our family.

Although my husband is now out of the military, we will forever remain connected to our military family. As we transitioned back to the civilian lifestyle, I spent a lot of time reflecting on the existence of nuclear missiles and their impacts from both the personal and global perspective. If I could snap my fingers and make all the world's nuclear missiles disappear, I would do it in a second. Unfortunately, a world completely free of nuclear weapons is no longer possible. It is possible, however, to use our knowledge and resources in a positive effort toward mankind. We need to take immediate steps toward a more globally optimistic maintenance of our resources and significantly reduce the number of nuclear weapons across the globe.

Somewhere along the course of my primary and secondary education, I became familiar with the atomic bombings on Hiroshima and Nagasaki, Japan in August of 1945. Learning a more detailed history of these events has been essential in determining my own stance in regard to nuclear missiles. Nuclear missiles are the result of a chain reaction discovered mainly by scientists Albert Einstein and Leo Szilard in the two decades prior to the bombings in Japan. The reaction is made possible by conversion of uranium to plutonium. Einstein and Szilard drafted a letter concerning their discoveries that was delivered to President Franklin Roosevelt in 1939. This all led to a program called the Manhattan Project that would produce the first nuclear missile. Their first nuclear missile device was tested in July of 1945 and a mere month later the United States carried out the bombings in Hiroshima and Nagasaki (Badash 138-48).

As one might imagine, there has been enormous skepticism and debate on the role these scientists played in the bombings on Japan. While we can never know exactly what was happening in the minds of these scientists, I believe that some motivation was based on good intentions. Dr. Charles Ferguson is the president of the Federation of American Scientists and an adjunct professor at Oxford University. His service as an officer on a nuclear submarine toward the end of the Cold War led him to study engineering at the Naval Nucler Power School. According to Dr. Ferguson, Einstein was persuaded by Leo Szilard, Edward Teller, and Eugene Wagner to lend his name in the letter to President Roosevelt although he "Did not, however, work on the Manhattan Project, which developed the first nuclear bombs" (22). It is also important to remember the global tensions of World War II at the time and the influence they may have had on these scientists. Regardless of their motives, the scientists made a discovery that would forever impact our world.

Learning the history and source of nuclear missiles made me realize that had these particular scientists not made this discovery, it would only have been a matter of time until others did. The fact that nuclear missiles indirectly come from a natural element makes it clear the problem lies not in the resources themselves, but in the methods upon which they are used. It was perhaps best put by Einstein as he said "What nature tells one group of men, she will tell in time to any group interested and patient enough in asking the questions" (1). The never-ending quest for knowledge and progress of mankind would undoubtedly have led to the discovery of this chain reaction in some way or another. The information may have taken a different route had someone other than Einstein or Szilard made the discovery, but the conversion of uranium to plutonium would still be a possibility to those willing to pursue. In order to move toward reduction of our nuclear missiles, it is important that each and every one of us take action to persuade these materials to be used in a positive manner. It is no secret that the materials are available to us, so we must accept this fact and move forward. Our job as members of society is to speak up about the well-being of our planet and its inhabitants. The negative use of our natural resources will only multiply if we allow it to multiply.

Unfortunately, the bombings of Hiroshima and Nagasaki were only the beginning to making nuclear weaponry. Negative actions can spread like wildfire, and they did just that during the Cold War. Other countries would eventually catch on to the production of these missiles. Dr. Ferguson's recent book on nuclear energy states that "In sum, the eight known possessors of nuclear weapons are China, France, India, North Korea, Pakistan, Russia, the United Kingdom, and the United States; the ninth undeclared nuclear arms possessor is Israel (107). While efforts have been made and treaties have been signed to determine the exact number each country has, we may never be certain that all the facts are on the table. We do know that the United States and Russia have drastically more missiles than any other country. In 2009, to the best of our knowledge, these two countries had a combined total of almost 10,000 nuclear missiles. France trailed in third with a mere estimate of 350 missiles (Ferguson 108). If these estimations don't make it clear that Russia and the United States have more missiles than necessary, consider the fact that "A successful first strike from Washington or Moscow would inflict catastrophic environmental damage that would make agriculture impossible and cause mass starvation" (Starr).

The United States and Russia have more than enough nuclear missiles to destroy all of civilization. Human security should not be insured by military might, but instead by appropriate distribution of resources, food, shelter, clean water, clean air, health care, and education (Starr). We deserve the right to feel protected by peace, rather than to feel protected by harmful, debilitating weapons. One individual cannot create world peace, but by taking positive action toward a more peaceful society we can certainly make a difference. As citizens we need to make our voices heard and demand for a reduction in our nuclear missiles. We are not demanding the impossible, but rather making it clear that we are aware of the unnecessary abundance of these missiles.

It is important to understand that although we have so many nuclear missiles, all they have done for decades is collect dust while requiring security and maintenance. The bombings on Hiroshima and Nagasaki remain the only active use of nuclear weapons in war. Their immense lasting effects have caused the world to consider nuclear missiles as more of a deterrent than anything else. Secretary-General of the United Nations Ban Ki-moon noted that nuclear weapons "Have been likened to a pair of scorpions in a bottle, each understanding that the first strike would be suicidal" (1). Scorpions, however, do not require the amount of security and maintenance that our nuclear missiles and their resources do. There are three U.S. Air Force Bases that maintain and operate the United States' nuclear missiles: Malmstrom AFB in Montana, F.E. Warren AFB in Wyoming, and Minot AFB in North Dakota. Between the three bases, there are approximately 9,180 total military and civilian personnel required to maintain and secure our nuclear missiles (www.af.mil). Some are quick to assume that this is a good thing as it creates many jobs for our economy, but it is important to realize what these jobs entail. My husband may have had to deal with a stagnant and demanding schedule, but we were fortunate as many have it much worse. A vast amount of these positions involve serious health risks; cancers, tumors, infertility, and genetic damage are among the plethora of side effects experienced from radiation exposure. I urge you to consider how many lives could be improved or even saved by a reduction in nuclear missiles across the globe. By choosing not to disarm nuclear missiles, we are ignoring the wellbeing of mankind.

"Massive arsenals capable of annihilating entire nations within an hour are more of a liability than an asset because they breed mistrust and worst-case assumptions among other states and perpetuate the risk of accidental or unauthorized launch" (Kimball 1). This quote really stands out to me, as I can recall my husband coming home with stories of random accidents or miscommunication. While the general public is certainly not aware of all the mishaps, it is important to understand that they do happen and any mishap in communication involving nuclear missiles could be the cause of a nuclear war. The Project of the Nuclear Age Peace Foundation lists a total of twenty mishaps involving the United States that could have, and in some cases almost did, lead to nuclear war (Starr). The more nuclear missiles we have, the greater the chance of false alarm that could lead to complete catastrophe. Nuclear missiles are a metastasizing tumor that must be treated before the cancer destroys our planet.

We must take responsibility in making sure that the cuts in nuclear stockpiles President Obama has proposed are taking place. When a nuclear weapon is retired, paperwork and dismantling must be done. These missiles were not made to be dismantled and therefore there is some concern as to the risk involved. It has been done, it is possible, and I am willing to bet the men and women who work with these missiles would rather take the risks knowing they are being dismantled than continue with the current situation. The time has come to take charge and put our efforts toward a positive cause; the longer we wait, the harder it will be.

While I can dream of a world peace in which there are no nuclear missiles in our future, the reality is that we may never see a world free of nuclear missiles again. What we can see is cooperation and a reduction in the mass number of nuclear missiles throughout the world. We are doing more than just causing health risks; nuclear missiles require unnecessary military expenditures, promote violent conflict, and reduce the availability of resources for social and economic development.

Being a military spouse across the country from my family at a young age caused me to constantly focus on the problems of nuclear missiles. It is a fair assumption to say that I was slightly bitter on the topic during the four years that my husband was consistently deployed to a MAF (missile alert facility) for five days at a time, with little or no exception to holidays and time off. It was not until after Josh got out of the military that I began to focus not on the problems, but on the solutions. Albert Einstein said himself that "The significant problems we face cannot be solved at the same level of thinking we were at when we created them" (1). We must challenge ourselves and work together to find solutions. Talk to your friends, family, and local representatives; make the fight toward a reduction in nuclear missiles and help create a better future.

## Works Cited

Badash, Lawrence. "American Physicists, Nuclear Weapons in World War II, and Social Responsibility." *Physics in Perspective* 7.2 (2005): 138-49. Print.

Ban Ki-moon. "Disarm Nuclear Weapons for Peace." *The Atlanta Journal - Constitution*: A.19. (2009). Print.

Einstein, Albert. "Albert Einstein." *Brainy Quote*. 2011. Web. 12 Oct. 2011.

Ferguson, Charles D. *Nuclear Energy*. New York: Oxford University Press, 2011. Print.

Kimball, Daryl G. "Getting Real about Nuclear Disarmament." Arms Control Today 38.3 (2008): 3. Print.

Starr, Steven. *Nuclear Files*. Nuclear Age Peace Foundation. 1998-2011. Web. 01 Dec. 2011.

United States Air Force. *F.E. Warren Air Force Base*. 01 Dec. 2011. Web. 01 Dec. 2011.

United States Air Force. *Malmstrom Air Force Base*. 03 Aug. 2010. Web. 01 Dec. 2011.

United States Air Force. *Minot Air Force Base*. 14 Apr. 2011. Web. 01 Dec. 2011.

Loyd Webb
WRT 150

A Golden Experience

On scaffolding standing fourteen feet tall next to The B.O.B., the Big Old Building in downtown Grand Rapids, stood two detailed gold sculptures of men. The crowd looked at these sculptures with confused looks on their faces. Both sculptures were dressed like construction workers wearing long work clothes, boots, a vest and a hard hat; all of which were real clothing material and the same gold color as their hands and faces. As I got closer, I could see what was puzzling the audience. One man was clearly a metal sculpture because it reflected the sunlight. The other man holding the rail looked as if it were a real man standing as still as the other sculpture! (See Appendix A). I could hear adults and children around me betting their friends and family that the sculpture holding the rail was a real man. I too was unsure and decided to get even closer to study them myself. Suddenly the sculpture holding the rail frightened the first few rows of the audience as it unfroze and began to talk. The man holding the rail is a living statue, making him both the artist *and* the art.

Lifetime resident of West Michigan, Robert Shangle, and his perfor-mance art piece *Under Construction* offered Art Prize goers a unique experi-ence which gave them a whole new perspective about performance art. He was able to relate his hometown and his artistic passion in this year's Art Prize performance. In West Michigan, things in the area are constantly changing, rebuilding, and improving. New buildings and parks are being built, new festivals are coming to town, and new people are joining the community ("LiveStatue and Friends" 1). An artist creates ideas and brings them to life through his or her art. This year, Shangle and a hand crafted statue suited up in construction worker clothes and were displayed on scaffolding with props such as traffic cones and lights to bring the scene to life. Designing this new art piece makes him seem as if he were a planner or an architect who designed a new building. Performing with his art piece makes him seem as if he were a construction worker bringing an artist's vision to life. Both of the roles he played not only gave his audience a new and an exciting type of performance art to observe, but also added a signifi-cant amount of depth behind the art piece's meaning.

*Loyd wrote his portfolio in the class of Sister Lucia Treanor, F.S.E.*

Shangle has been preforming as LiveStatue, his human statue performance name, for many years now. It was no surprise that he received ninth place in the 2011 Art Prize competition. From performing in Art Prize for three years now to representing the USA at the 2009 LivingStatue World Championship in the Netherlands in front of 350,000 spectators, he is both a local and an international expert of this demanding art form (Estep 1). He believes he acquired his mental and physical toughness to perform this art form from running track and field at Aquinas College in Grand Rapids, and from running in several ultra-marathons after graduation. In an interview with Shangle, he explained that his techniques to prepare both mentally and physically for these grueling races have correlated with his ability to obtain high endurance for various static positions. His endurance and fascination with the human body had led him to research and utilize ways to quickly slower his heart rate and gain control his breathing (Shangle). Years of experience and knowledge of the human body allow him to get in "the zone" and perform for hours at a time with very little noticeable movements (Seites 1). He has mastered an art form popular in Europe and has brought it back to the United States share his discovery with those who want to take the time to understand it. His interaction with the audience and specific choice of color has drawn many to this non-domestic style of performance art.

"I've had people two feet from me debating whether I am a statue. I will wink at the other one, and they will scream." said Shangle two years ago on an interview with the *Grand Rapids Press* (Estep 1). At that time, he had been practicing for the 2009 LivingStatue World Championship in the Netherlands on a sidewalk in downtown Grand Rapids by startling those who passed by (See Appendix B). If he can become static for hours on end, then why would he have wanted to scare and talk to those who passed by? After all, wouldn't performing mean holding a continuous static position? This is because this type of performance art is based on a living person who can give viewers more than they expect. Shangle normally performs by himself and occasionally with a few props (See Appendix C). This year, he created a real statue to have someone to perform with. With one statue being an actual statue and the other statue being a real human being, his audience questioned themselves which one is which. This is what drew them into his art.

Shangle has added his own variation to the style of this performance art, increasing his ability to draw in his audience while maintaining his static illusion. In Europe, this art form is more respected and widespread. The whole display at which an artist performs is usually more elaborate; the poses are held longer and then a choreographed skit is performed when he or she is in motion. Artists typically wear sunglasses or keep their eyes closed while static as it is hard to keep your eye lids open for long periods of time. In America, this art form is relatively new and therefore unanticipated, giving the artist more opportunities to amaze their unexpecting viewers. For this reason, Shangle performs static positions less than performers in Europe would, giving him more opportunities to not only scare and excite his audience, but to spread the knowledge about living statues as well. He has trained and developed his eyes to keep open for an extended period of time. This ability helps create the illusion of a real statue at any distance from the audience, decreasing the likelihood that his victims will tell him apart from his statue and increasing his chance to frighten them. Although he has the ability freeze frame for several hours at a time, Shangle states that "quite frankly, that would be boring." (Shangle).

When he unfreezes and begins to talk to his audience, he astonishes his viewers who are already drawn into it. While observing him myself at Art Prize, he unfroze and told all the children to come to the front of the audience. He wanted them to mimic his actions by extending their arms and holding a thumbs up position with their hands on the count of three. When he counted to three, he instantly froze in that position as the children struggled to keep their arms from moving. I joined the crowd as they cheered him on. This interaction with the audience and more importantly the children is what drew many to the scene as he performed ("Under Construction"). His audience of all ages entertains him as much as he entertains them. He loves to see them smile and to hear their comments as well as to frighten them and to make them laugh. His ability to positively communicate with his audience fits very well with the objective of this type of performance art (Shangle).

Shangle is static for a majority of the time when he performs, exhibiting a more plastic arts aspect rather than a performance art aspect. When he interacts with the crowd and moves around, he exhibits more of a theatrical aspect. The line between the boundaries of performance art and theatre seems to be in flux at times of his performance. Shangle believes that living statue performance is sort of a mixture of both facets. Statue display is artistic because it has to stand up and exhibit a theme and meaning. He believes that performance art has many theatrical elements and they occur when the performers move and connect with the audience (Shangle). Combining the elements of both performance art and theatre allow him to produce art pieces that are especially unique to viewers as together they show that art has no boundaries on the creative minds of artists.

In a recent interview with the *Grand Rapids Press*, Shangle stated that he is happy to have shared something unique with Art Prize. He believes a lot of people look at performance artists as street performers and do not consider it to be a real form of art. He wants to introduce and educate West Michigan and the whole United States that this is in fact a true form of art that has been around for many years. It has taken a couple years for the United States to see this as art, but he hopes that we have enjoyed it ("The Grand Rapids Press").

Living Statues have been around as a form of entertainment for over a hundred years. In the 1840s, the showman PT Barnum was known for his display of Living Statues as a part of his collection of circus performances. In the 1960s, Gilbert and George, who believed the entertainment value of living statues was debatable, took on a different approach by strictly containing them within a gallery to be viewed. Little is known about the origins of Living Statue performance for any use. This art seemed to have appeared suddenly in Europe at some period in the late 2000s and soon spread all over the world. Today they can be found in most major cities and towns in all shapes, sizes, and colors (Johnson 2).

On the Discovery Channel's science entertainment television show *MythBusters*, hosts Adam Savage and Jamie Hyneman conducted an experiment to test the Goldfinger myth, stating that covering the body in gold paint can be fatal by skin asphyxiation like in the James Bond movie Goldfinger. After about an hour and a half of being covering in gold paint from head to toe, Jamie began to experience a slight and temporary flu-like feeling and an increase in blood pressure, but was not afflicted with any major illness (Pilot 1). When Shangle was asked if he ever experiences these symptoms, he clarified that he in fact does not use paint of any kind on his skin, but rather a special order theatrical makeup with the same appearance as gold paint. I am not sure whether or not he believes in the myth, but the theatrical makeup does not make him feel any adverse symptoms (Shangle).

Painting one's self gold may seem to be an extreme for some viewers, but the symbolism of the color gold is what makes this piece of art stand out even more. Gold has many more meanings than just the modern day typical assumption of wealth. In The Holy Bible, gold has been depicted as an item to show reverence to God as it was used to make the Ark of the Covenant to hold the Ten Commandments and was one of the three gifts presented to Jesus at his birth (Exodus 30.; Matthew 1.). The best performing athletes in the Olympics receive gold medals after achieving first place, signifying their dominance over all the other competition in an event. Gold in the form of jewelry and other expensive items can simply represent happiness, success, love, and wealth, but Shangle's use of the color is even more simple than I had expected.

Shangle's use of the color gold is primarily because of how well it benefits him when performing. He has experimented with various colors throughout his career, eventually discovering that the color gold looks best in different lighting. Art Prize is a unique venue because it requires a sufficient amount of sunlight to effectively display all the art work. Shangle found white, marble colors to look "ghostly" at night, and dark iron, steel colors to look flat and non-metallic under cloudy skies. The gold, copper like color he allows him to maintain his static illusion and perform at the venue under the conditions of sunlight, cloudiness, twilight, and nightfall with artificial lighting (Shangle). The color adds to his performance capabilities and makes it even more dynamic as it stands out amongst the other artwork around him. It is a color that many do not see on everyday basis, easily drawing in the wandering eyes of those who pass by. It does not only make it convenient for him to perform in varies atmospheric conditions, but also allows him to remain static and let the audience come to him.

It was simply an honor to have someone with such a unique artistic ability discuss with me his passion. Under Construction was more than just an entertaining performance art piece. It was a statement to viewers not only about West Michigan, but also about keeping their own eyes open for new changes occurring around them. I stumbled upon Shangle's art piece unaware of any significance it might have held. Looking back on the day I was in the audience, I was drawn into his art by all the reasons he had set out for people to be drawn by; the most substantial being his interaction and entertainment with the children. My reaction to this art piece may be influenced by the fact that I had never seen a performance like Shangle's before and that I rarely take the time to mentally evaluate art at all. However, this performance art is not an easy one to accomplish, but Shangle clearly loves what he does and I believe that is what art is all about.

## Works Cited

Estep, Darin. "Did that statue just wink? Sparta resident Robert Shangle tests talent at World Living Statue Championships." Mlive.com. 17 Aug. 2009. Web. 10 Oct. 2011.

The Grand Rapids Press, dir. "Robert Shangle discusses crowd interaction." Mlive.com. Michigan Live LLC, 30 Sep. 2011. Interview. 18 Oct. 2011.

Gonzalez, John. "'LivingStatue' artist Robert Shangle returns to ArtPrize at The B.O.B." *Mlive.com.* Michigan Live LLC, 23 Sept. 2010. Web. 29 Nov. 2011.

The Holy Bible: King James Version. New York: American Bible Society, 2000. Print.

Johnson, Ed. "The Living Statue Company – Living Statue Resource Page." *The Living Statue Company.* 2008. Web. 2 Dec. 2011.

"LiveStatue and Friends." Art Prize. 9 Oct. 2011. Web. 10 Oct. 2011.

"Pilot 3: Larry's Lawn Chair Balloon, Poppy Seed Drug Test, Goldfinger." MythBuster Results. 7 March 2003. Web. 1 Dec. 2011.

Seites, Doug. "Featured Alumnus: Robert Shangle '90". Aquinas College. Web. 10 Oct. 2011.

Shangle, Robert. Personal interview. 20 Oct. 2011.

Under Construction. By Robert Shangle. The Big Old Building, Grand Rapids. 4 Oct. 2011. Live Performance.

**Appendix A**

Fig. 1 The man holding the rail, Robert Shangle, and his sculpture "LiveStatue and Friends.").

**Appendix B**

Fig. 2 Robert Shangle in downtown Grand Rapids preparing for his next victim. Taken by Rex Larsen (Espen).

**Appendix C**

Fig. 3 Robert Shangle at Art Prize 2010 with a camera as a prop (Gonzalez).

Loyd Webb
WRT 150

Eye on the Prize

Bang! We raced out of the blocks! One hurdle after another we flew down the lane hoping to eventually gain the lead towards the end. I was in fourth place and knew only the top three made it to the finals. In a battle with the two hurdlers in front of me, I knew it was time pick up the pace and take the lead. I felt the wind against my back quickly pushing me over the last two hurdles, positioning me in front my competition and into second place. I ran across the finish line and clenched my fists as I held my arms up in celebration. I was going to the finals! I could hear my team cheering my name from the top of the bleachers.

"Loyd!" Antonio's loud voice quickly took me out of my trance.

"Huh? What?"

"Go! What the hell are you waiting for? We don't have all day!"

"Right! Sorry!"

I ran to the line and positioned my right foot just before it and left foot about three feet behind it. I bent my knees and leaned forward as I looked down the lane at the first hurdle, thinking about the first step I would take as soon as I heard the word. . .

"Go!"

Before I knew it, I had already gone over the first hurdle, and counting my steps as I came down to the ground, I quickly approached the second hurdle. "One, two, three… four?" I counted in my head as I awkwardly ran over the second hurdle with the wrong lead leg. My right leg went over as my left foot hooked onto the bar, causing me to tumble hard onto my right side. I braced myself for what I always received after I screwed up a practice drill.

"Loyd!" said an even louder and deeper voice as I picked myself up off the ground.

"Remember what I told you? You gotta get your beginning steps to the first hurdle down or else you will not be able to do three steps in between the rest of them! Go back and do it again!"

He took off his cap, wiped the sweat off his bald head with his right sleeve, and walked onto the football field as he watched the four by two hundred meter relay team practice their baton hand offs. Even he was sweating on that scorching hot afternoon and all he had been doing was watching us run around a track a million times. We were less than 24 hours away from the state meet and my coach still had time to yell at me.

Coach Randy Williams was a tall, long legged man with a slightly round gut. He always stood upright, never slouching, making his shoulders as broad as he was bold. He occasionally wore his army uniform when we were in for a hard practice to add to his intimidating figure. When he talked, he paced back and forth as his black army boots thumped the ground beneath him. His mind spoke words of wisdom as his deep voice projected those words into our ears. He was straight-faced most of the time, but at heart he was as kind and caring as a father. His witty humor was what kept us going on the hardest days of the season; through struggles both on and off the track. The most unique quality about him was that he seemed to have a relative story for every problematic situation in life. These stories ranged from his own experiences in track and field to stories about his deployment to the war in Iraq. They gave us an insight on the man's motivational life which inspired our will to better our own.

I brushed myself off, turned around, and looked at Antonio as I walked back to the starting line. He had a slight grin on his face which made me curious as to what he was about to say.

"What?" I asked him in a suspicious tone.

"Couldn't see the hurdle?" he replied in a friendly, joking matter.

I chuckled and rolled my eyes at his attempt to lighten the mood.

He tried again. "Don't you roll your eye at me!"

We both broke out in laughter almost to the point of tears. He and I always enjoyed making jokes about my eye condition. When I was twelve months old, I was diagnosed with cancer of the retina on my right eye. It was too late to save my eye, but I am fortunate enough to have my life at the cost of having a fake, glass eye. Anyone who knows me is aware that I openly joke about it all the time, and anyone who was as close to me as Antonio knows exactly how to make me laugh even if I did not want to. He was like a brother to me because we always tried to help each other become better hurdlers while avidly competing in the same events to beat each other.

I returned to the line and finished up my drills as Antonio ran barefoot on the blistering track for his cool down. The heat had started to get to me and I had begun to feel exhausted, so I decided to lie down on the cool, watered grass of the infield. I closed my eyes and felt a calm breeze against my perspiring face, once again visualizing what the following day would be like. I saw myself at the finish line of the final heat of the one hundred and ten meter high hurdle race. I had come in first place, beating Antonio by just a few of milliseconds. I was glistening with sweat and tired past the point of exhaustion, but the feeling was so profound. The roaring sound of the three thousand or so people cheering as we both became state qualifying hurdlers was a feeling like none other I had ever experienced. I was then awoken from my daydream by a tall, dark figure with a loud, booming voice.

"How ya feelin, baby?" Coach Randy asked as he held out his hand to help me up.

"I'm all right. Just tired." I replied as I was yanked up off the ground.

"Good, good! The coaches and I are having a good feeling about this one! You have to get your head in the game and give it all you got."

"I'll do my best, Coach." I replied with a little bit of assurance as I nodded my head.

We left the track, headed back to the hotel and rested up for the biggest day of the season. I found it quite difficult to sleep that night. I kept wondering whether or not I would really have the ability to make my vision become a reality.

The next morning we woke up bright and early, eager to get to the track and see what we could accomplish. We went to the lobby and huddled together as Coach Randy led us in a prayer and gave a quick speech. He never really gave quick speeches, so this one made him seem just as eager to go as we were.

"Guys…This is it. You know what we came here to do. I'm not looking for anything more than for all you guys to do your best. And I mean your very best. This will not be an easy meet by any means, so go out there and show those teams that you know how to compete on their level. We have had the best season in school history, so let's go and finish it off strong!"

We all clapped and cheered and started to get pumped up as we moved closer into the huddle.

"Falcons on three!" Coach Randy yelled with enthusiasm.

We all shouted "One, two, three, Falcons!" and then we were on our way. When we arrived, I could feel the warming energy in the atmosphere the moment I stepped off the bus. Since the preliminary high hurdle race is one of the first events, Antonio and I had to go over to the starting line and check in before the meet actually started. We received our hip numbers and began to stretch out and warm up. Antonio began to limp as he jogged around, so I approached him to see what was going on. His feet were badly burned from running barefoot on the hot track the previous day at practice. He went over to the coaching staff and explained his injury to see what could be done about it. As I was warming up, Coach Randy came over to me with a blank expression on his face.

"Antonio can't run. We have someone to fill in for his four by two hundred meter relay, but you will be the only one running the one hundred and ten meter hurdle race."

He saw that the news put me in a state of unease, so he continued to talk.

"I know you sometimes don't fully have your heart at the track, and I know sometimes you don't want to be here running around it all the time, but you have talent, Man! Some people have dedicated more time than you have in the past ten years in track and still aren't as good as you! And sometimes it kills me to see you slacking off because I know you are so much better than that! I'm not saying you're the best person out here and should win, but I am saying that you need to do what we both know you can do. So what are you waiting for? Go by the starting line and get ready. You're in heat three, lane six."

He then turned around and walked up the ramp to the top of the bleachers. That is the first time I had actually been preached to and felt like he truly cared about me. I felt like he had given me true fatherly advice, seeing as mine was not around all the time. I went to the starting line and watched the first and second heats go. Before I knew it, I was taking off my sweats and standing in my uniform ready for the official to say. . .

"On your marks!"

All eight of us in the heat got down on our knees, took our positions in the blocks, and placed our fingers before the line. I looked to my left and spotted the favored high hurdler of the year in lane four. It didn't bother me that he was in my heat, but seeing him made me realize how hard I would have to push myself to win this race.

"Get set!"

We all raised our rear ends and waited for the sound of the gun. I felt my arms shaking as I desperately tried to prevent my adrenaline filled body from running out before the sound. Bang! We exploded out of the blocks! I made the first hurdle perfectly and the second just the same. I was cruising down the lane, focusing on nothing else but running over the next hurdle in front of me. As I approached the eighth hurdle, the wind picked up and the most astonishing event happened to me as I ran over it. My eye came right out of my socket and flew behind me! I could hear all three thousand or so spectators gasp as my eye soared all the way from lane six into lane three. That had never happened to me in the ten years I had ran track and what better day to have that happen than the state meet. It took me by surprise and threw me off my rhythm as I came down and approached the ninth hurdle. I ran over the last two hurdles slower than the others and finished in fourth place, missing the last qualifying position by one place. I stood at the finish line with one eye and laughed along with my team and Coach Randy who I could hear all the way from the track to the top of the bleachers. I received my time from the scores table, retrieved my eye which had somehow found its way into lane two by then, and walked back to get my things by the starting line. As funny as that moment was, I wondered what Coach Randy was really thinking about the outcome of the race.

"In all my years of track and field," Coach Randy said as I approached him and the rest of the coaching staff, "I have never seen anything like that during a race!"

I knew that was a priceless moment that I could never forget, but I still could not stop thinking about whether or not Coach Randy actually cared that I did not place in the top three to qualify for the finals. He put his hand on my shoulder, walked me away from the rest of the team and staff, and began to talk to me.

"I'm proud of what you did out there. That is the effort I knew you were capable of all along."

"I had the lead and I know I could have placed in the top three if that fluke had not happened."

He looked shocked as if I should not have said that.

"I told you to do your best today, not to win a medal. Yes, I know you could have placed within the top three because your effort proved it. Your condition has nothing to do with hindering your success. Your previous lack of effort is what was doing that."

That is when I had finally figured it out; why I kept getting preached at by not only Coach Randy, but also my mother when I had not done things to my full potential. I did not win a state title and that may or may not have been inhibited by my eye condition, but I could have had more attempts at earning a state title other than just my senior year of high school if I had put forth effort that reflected my will to achieve it in previous years. That is when I believed I have great potential to achieve what I want the most if I put all my effort into achieving my goals. If I had gotten that far with little or no effort, what could I possibly be capable of if I give my all in that everything I do? And it is not even just for track and field; it is also school, family problems and those everyday hurdles I have to get over. That unexpected event triggered a much needed revelation before going onto college. Although more than half of my life had been defined by track and field, I chose that it was not what I truly wanted to continue doing with my spare time and energy. Now I choose to focus on the equivalent or even much more difficult goal of being a medical doctor rather than an Olympic athlete. What I learned about myself that day at the state track meet gave me a story that I can pass on to others just like the ones Coach Randy passed onto me.

Loyd Webb
WRT 150

Manual Mutiny

In general, a person who is suffering from pain or an illness sees a medical physician in search of a cure. Before the physician uses medical equipment to locate the cause of his or her patient's illness, he or she will use their eyes, hands, and ears to aid them in finding symptoms that can be detected without the use of advanced technology. Similarly, a person who is suffering from psychological illness sees a mental health professional who will help guide them to a more mentally stable lifestyle. The difference between the two is that psychological disorders are far more difficult for mental health professionals to diagnose, as both the symptoms and the illnesses reside mostly in the brain. This fact in itself poses a major problem for this field of health. The diagnosis of a mental illness requires mental health professionals to undergo rigorous clinical training in order to apply proper and effective methods of psychotherapy to their patients as well as to prevent diagnostic and treatment errors. They have no concrete way of knowing exactly what disorder or symptoms a patient might have because they can only use their patient's actions and descriptions of problems as diagnostic material.

For this reason, the American Psychiatric Association (APA) took the initiative of drafting the first edition of the Diagnostic and Statistical Manual of Mental Disorders (DSM-I) in 1952 to provide the mental health community with a common language and standard criteria for the classification of mental disorders ("Post-World" 1). This edition and the second edition (DSM-II) are both relatively short manuals that provided only a brief description of each psychiatric disorder. These editions attempted to apply a universal diagnostic standard for many psychological disorders, but failed to provide enough information for clinicians to accept their reliability and to trust their validity. The development and release of the third edition of the manual (DSM-III) marked the beginning of a determined effort by the APA to increase the reliability and validity of the DSM by connecting assigned diagnostic claims to research data rather than simply the consensus of APA members (Beutler 4). The DSM-III and its revised edition (DSM-III-R) were both criticized by clinicians for many different reasons, the most substantial being their exclusion of psychologists, social workers, and other mental health professional's contribution to the diagnosis and treatment in psychopathology. This criticism followed with the publication of the fourth and current edition of the manual (DSM-IV) and its text revision (DSM-IV-TR) (5-6).

The fifth edition of the manual (DSM-5) that has been projected to be released in 2013 has already stirred the minds of many mental health professional groups including the American Psychological Association, the Society of Biological Psychiatry, the American Counseling Association, and the British Psychological Society. Several divisions of the American Psychological Association have written an open letter to the DSM-5 Task Force of the American Psychiatric Association (APA) responding to their proposed changes that will be made and regarding the grave dangers they will bring. From reckless expansion of the diagnostic system to lack of scientific rigor, much has been said about where the direction of this edition is headed, but the APA fails to see why a secluded manual can cause devastating results that could potentially affect far more than just a patient's health (Frances, Psychologists 1). Although the DSM is the sole property of the APA, members should allow mental health professionals to contribute to the drafting of the DSM-5, and review their proposed changes to the current manual, creating a more reliable and valid resource that will help prevent false-positive diagnoses of mental illnesses and reflect positively on the field of psychiatry.

The DSM-5 Task Force should be commended for its efforts to update the manual in response to the growing body of scientific knowledge on psychological distress and new empirical research data obtained after a decade. Many studies have been conducted in those years and the APA found that it is beneficial to produce a new manual for its many users to accurately categorize and diagnose mental illnesses with. Its effort in addressing limitations to the reliability of the current categorical system of illnesses is much appreciated by the American Psychology Association and many other professional organizations as well. The prevalent issue with the drafting of the DSM-5 is that the APA has yet to realize that the reliability of the manual will only increase with the contribution of other professional groups.

The DSM-III and DSM-IV had received heavy criticism for that same issue of excluding the contribution of many professional groups. The DSM is the rightful property of the APA and has been since the DSM-I, but this does not grant it any special mandate giving it any sovereignty over psychiatric diagnosis. The exclusion of many well-respected mental health professional groups leads them to believe the APA thinks it can set the standards for psychiatric disorders, making its reliability hard to be completely accepted by these groups. The manual has become a primary resource used by psychiatrists, psychologists, and other medical practitioners, as well as for forensics, health insurance practice, and public policy for many different reasons ("Open" 1). When it comes down to defining a specific mental illness, professionals find it socially acceptable to refer to the manual as a reliable resource that can provide consistent results for cases that are similar. If this is true, it should also be that information solely provided by a specialized task force of a single professional group could not possibility be as reliable and efficient in properly categorizing and diagnosing mental illnesses than the contribution of the mental health professional field as a whole.

The DSM-5 Task Force's proposed changes to the DSM-IV-TR for the DSM-5 are frightening these professional groups, making them question its reliability even more. They are proposing to widen the range of the diagnostic system for multiple illnesses. This will decrease the limitations at which practitioners have to diagnose illnesses with and will cause more people to fall within the criteria for illnesses. According to the American Psychology Association's open letter to the DSM-5 Task Force, the lowering of diagnostic thresholds is scientifically premature and holds numerous risks ("Open" 2). Sensitivity in diagnosing illnesses is important in order to establish limitations for illnesses and to prevent false-positive diagnoses. If the number of people who qualify for an illness is increased by the lack of diagnostic sensitivity, then the increase of over diagnosing and excessive medicalization is almost certain.

Proposals for lowering the diagnostic thresholds for behavioral illnesses such as Social Anxiety Disorder and Attention Deficit Hyperactivity Disorder (ADHD) contain examples of slight changes that could have a variety of effects on patients who are diagnosed with them. These types of changes are evident in the beginning criteria for Social Anxiety Disorder. As stated in the DSM-IV-TR, Criterion A and B for Social Anxiety Disorder read:

> A marked and persistent fear of one or more social or performance situations in which the person is exposed to unfamiliar people or to possible scrutiny by others. The individual fears that he or she will act in a way (or show anxiety symptoms) that will be humiliating or embarrassing [Criterion A]. Exposure to the feared social situation almost invariably provokes anxiety, which may take the form of a situationally bound or situationally predisposed Panic Attack [Criterion B]. ("300.23" 4).

This is telling the reader that Social Anxiety Disorder is most likely to reside with a person who frequently experiences the fear of social or performance situations which consistently evokes anxiety to them. The criteria are very detailed and goes into even more detail past Criterion B. The APA's proposed revisions for Criterion A and B for Social Anxiety Disorder reads:

Marked fear or anxiety about one or more social situations in which the person is exposed to possible scrutiny by others. Examples include social interactions (e.g., having a conversation), being observed (e.g., eating or drinking), or performing in front of others (e.g., giving a speech) [Criterion A]. The individual fears that he or she will act in a way, or show anxiety symptoms, that will be negatively evaluated (i.e., be humiliating, embarrassing, lead to rejection, or offend others) [Criterion B]. ("E 04" 1).

They are proposing the exclusion of the word "persistent" in the description of Criterion A, reducing the severity constraint and allowing more people to qualify for the illness. They also want to remove the phase "almost invariably provokes anxiety" from Criterion B, additionally lowering the frequency at which fear due to anxiety can be experienced. Both of these exclusions and many more to following criteria lower the diagnostic threshold and allow people who may not exactly have the illness to become trapped into being diagnosed with it.

Lowering the diagnostic thresholds for behavioral illnesses could be especially harmful for children. The symptoms of Social Anxiety Disorder are similar to being shy or freezing up when it comes to public speaking (Lane 2). If one of the criterions gives the fear of public speaking as an example in the manual, then it is extremely likely that numerous children will be diagnosed with the illness and medicated to treat it because many children frequently experience this fear. Kate Fallon, General Secretary of Britain's Association of Educational Psychologists, tells us that a shy child could be diagnosed with social anxiety disorder and a temporarily withdrawn child could be diagnosed with depression. These conditions are almost likely to be treated with medication. She states that under these circumstances, "we will be putting potent drugs into children with little or no understanding of what it will lead to." (3). This is not a statement to be taken lightly. Clinicians would prescribe these harmful drugs to children even without the parents knowing that they in fact will be playing a part in administering harmful drugs to their children daily.

The DSM-5 Task Force should be applauded for its efforts in making the manual's categorical system a more valid way of distinguishing between different illnesses. According to the DSM-5 Task Force, its work groups are considering the use of dimensional assessments as an additional way to help clinicians capture the symptoms and severity of mental illnesses. These dimensional assessments will give clinicians a systematic approach to evaluating patients on the full range of symptoms they may be experiencing ("Frequently"). Although this new systematic approach is very well constructed, it lacks scientific validity behind its claims. These claims for the treatment of mental illnesses seem to have very little reasoning behind how scientists came to the conclusions they are proposing. Etiology is the study of causation or origination, a study revered by the medical field as being an essential part in the discovery and treatment of illnesses. This approach would seem to be more demanding in the mental health field as professionals strive to treat an illness by getting down to the root of the problem rather than just treating its symptoms.

The DSM by design is primarily concerned with just the treatment aspect of psychotherapy rather than etiological based research because it only provides criteria and definitions of illnesses to diagnose patients with. The treatment of a mental illness is a risky task when not much is understood scientifically about the origin of the illness to begin with. According to the American Psychology Association, growing evidence suggests that psychotropic medications do not necessarily correct chemical imbalances and ultimately pose a substantial amount of adverse effects. Antipsychotic medications, for example, have been shown to have beneficial short term effects, but hold numerous long term risks including: obesity, diabetes, movement disorders, cognitive decline, worsening of psychotic symptoms, reduction in brain volume, and shortened lifespan. Neurobiology cannot fully explain the etiology of DSM-defined disorders, but a significant amount of evidence suggests that the brain is dramatically altered due to psychiatric treatment ("Open" 4-5).

The DSM-5 Task Force's experience with the DSM-IV should offer as a lesson and a precaution for what it is currently proposing. Chairman of the DSM-IV Task Force Allen Frances admitted to the DSM-IV being "an unwitting contributor to three false positive epidemics." (Frances, "The first draft" 1). The publication of the DSM-IV concurred with high rates of ADHD, autistic disorder, and childhood bipolar disorders. He states that the direction of the DSM-5's proposed slight changes "could potentially set off at least eight new false positive epidemics of psychiatric disorder." (2). The five disorders of binge eating, mixed anxiety depression, minor neurocognitive problem risk of psychosis, and temper dysregulation are already common in the general public, but will soon be defined by non-specific symptoms. The three existing disorders of ADHD, bipolar disorder, and major depressive disorder will have their already over-inclusive diagnostic thresholds lowered. Links can also be found between these eight disorders which would further increase the risk of over diagnosing a patient even more. Concluding the article, Frances admits that the ubiquitous marketing efforts of drug companies directed at doctors and the general public contributed to these epidemics (2-4). This statement makes me question the ethical principles of psychiatrists and clinicians, but the field should not be attacked in any way for being subject to malpractice.

The mental health field is a growing body of professionals which strives to treat illnesses that are afflicting patients. The DSM-5 is simply trying to achieve what the whole field is aiming to do. The DSM-5 Task Force and the members of the APA need to realize that this goal is much more achievable by setting aside the career labels of mental health professionals and working together as a team. Collaboration between the whole field will prevent false-positive diagnoses of mental illnesses and will provide the users of the DSM with a more reliable and valid resource. As a psychology student who is very concerned the field, this is a very real issue to me. If the DSM-5 Task Force fails to reconsider their proposals, I may ultimately change my career path to a medical field with less controversy. The psychiatry field has been a long-time interest of mine, but its reputation among other mental health professions makes me believe it will experience turmoil in the future. It is only a matter of time before the new manual will be used to diagnose patients. We can only hope that someday we will not fall into being a part of an epidemic.

## Works Cited

"300.23 Social Phobia (Social Anxiety Disorder)." *Diagnostic and Statistical Manual of Mental Disorders: DSM-IV-TR.* 4th ed. Washington, DC: American Psychiatric Association, 2000. Print.

Beutler, Larry E, and Mary L. Malik. *Rethinking the DSM: A Psychological Perspective.* Washington, DC: American Psychological Association, 2002. Print.

"E 04 Social Anxiety Disorder (Social Phobia)." DSM-5 Development. American Psychiatric Association, 2010. Web. 9 November 2011.

Frances, Allen J. "Psychologists Start Petition Against DSM 5." *Psychology Today.* Sussex Directories, Inc., 24 Oct. 2011. Web. 31 Oct. 2011.

Frances, Allen J. "The first draft of DSM-V." *British Medical Journal* (2010): 1-2. Web. 10 November 2011.

"Frequently Asked Questions." DSM-5 Development. American Psychiatric Association, 2010. Web. 9 November 2011.

Lane, Christopher. "DSM-5 Is Almost Certain to Expand the Criteria for Social Anxiety Disorder." *Psychology Today.* Sussex Directories, Inc., 9 Oct. 2011. Web. 31 Oct. 2011.

"Open Letter to the DSM-5." *Ipetitions.* Society for Humanistic Psychology. Web. 31 Oct. 2011.

"Post-World War II." *American Psychiatric Association.* 2011. Web. 31 Oct. 2011.

# Good Writing Around Campus

The main purpose of the first-year writing requirement is to prepare students for the academic and professional writing they will do after their freshman year. In this section, we highlight some quality writing completed in classes beyond WRT 150. By examining some of the other pieces that were written outside of WRT 150, you will observe a wider variety of topics, styles, and forms.

The following section contains pieces written by students in GVSU courses, some of which required WRT 150 as a prerequisite. **Allison Bogle** composed "A Brief Overview of American Homeschooling: A Guide for Parents" in "Liberal Studies Senior Seminar" (LIB 495) under the guidance of her professor, Phyllis Vandenberg. **Ian McNabb** wrote "The European Singularity" in Professor Edward Cole's course "European Civilization II" (HNR 225). **Josh Lycka** created "Women Write the Gulag and the Siege of Leningrad" in Professor Christine Rydel's course "Gulag in Siege/Leningrad" (HNR 311 SWS).

As you read, think about the form and content of each piece. How do the writers organize, develop, and support their essays? How have these writers learned to manipulate purpose and focus to convey information in an informative and meaningful way to their academic audience?

Allison Bogle
LIB 495

A Brief Overview of American Homeschooling: A Guide for Parents

## Introduction

Education is an important part of growing up and preparation for citizenship. There are many choices available for parents and children, including public, private, and home education. Every child learns differently, and what works for one child may not work for another. Homeschooling may be a viable option for parents and children that desire a unique educational experience. Modern homeschooling is a fairly young practice, with much of its history contained in the last fifty years. Parents choose to homeschool for many different reasons, and the practice has many advantages and disadvantages. Additionally, homeschooling is a controversial issue, especially the regulation of the practice. The goal of this paper is to provide a brief overview of American homeschooling, as well as to act as a guide for parents considering the practice.

## Historical Background of American Homeschooling

In the United States, children were not always taught in schools. Historically, children were educated in the home (Dumas 68). In fact, "the first education law in our country's history entrusted the education of children to their parents" (Dumas 68). According to author Brian D. Schwartz, a lack of public schools in the 1800s forced parents to educate their children at home; some wealthier parents hired private tutors or sent their children to private schools (Schwartz 5). However, during the common school movement, education shifted from the home to the public school (Spring 78). This shift took place in the 1830s and 1840s and changed the face of American education forever because and educational responsibilities shifted from the parents to the school teachers (Spring 37, 78). As a result of the shift toward public schools, the number of homeschooled students began to decline in the late 1800s (Schwartz 5). In 1852, "the first modern compulsory education statute was passed in Massachusetts" (Schwartz 5). This law required that all children of a certain age attend school, and thus, ended a parent's right to educate at home (Schwartz 5). Parents did not take this shift lightly. Many court cases resulted from the regulation of American education; however in this brief overview of homeschooling, all of the cases cannot be discussed.

The United States Supreme Court has yet to rule on a case exclusively regarding the constitutionality of homeschooling (Cooper 116). However, 1925's Pierce v. Society of Sisters was an important case for homeschoolers because it paved the way for today's home education laws. Pierce v. Society of Sisters did not specifically deal with the issue of homeschooling; it was actually a case about the right to send one's children to private school (Catholic private school in particular) (Schwartz 8). In Pierce v. Society of Sisters the United Stated Supreme Court determined that "in applying its compulsory education laws, a state cannot limit the authority of parents by mandating that all children attend public school" (Schwartz 8). Although Pierce v. Society of Sisters did not apply directly to home based education, it again allowed "parents to direct the educational upbringing of their children" (Schwartz 8). Essentially, Pierce v. Society of Sisters made it possible to entertain the idea of homeschooling children. The current home based education movement owes quite a bit to the impact of Pierce v. Society of Sisters.

Homeschooling of the current era (1960s to present) is quite different from the home education that took place at the birth of our country. "The home-based education of the past was nearly always done for pragmatic rather than ideological reasons" (Gaither 331). Parents of the past home-schooled out of necessity; however, parents from the modern movement seem to educate at home for more personal reasons. Many factors contributed to the popularity of the homeschool movement when it first began; however, feminism had much to do with it. According to author Milton Gaither, "the homeschooling movement cannot be understood apart from the dramatic rise in female education and political participation that the feminist movement has secured" (Gaither 334-335). The feminist movement gave women the right to choose to have a career, stay home, or both. However, women were college educated during this era and needed to find a place to apply their education (Gaither 335). Homeschooling became "a means for women who believe they should stay at home to nevertheless put their educational experience and talents to good use" (Gaither 335).

Homeschooling allowed mothers to educate their children and thus, legitimized their status as 'homemakers.'

Furthermore, politics played an important role in the emergence of the current homeschool movement. Gaither states that, "by the 1970s many young Americans had on both the left and the right had largely given up on building a better America, hoping instead to 'build alternative institutions and create alternative families – a separate, authentic, parallel universe'" (Gaither 335). This was the perfect breeding ground for homeschooling, because it allowed people on both ends of the political spectrum to customize their children's education in a way that goes against the government. Homeschooling became a form of protest.

In the early 1970s communes gained popularity, as did the free-wheeling counterculture. Liberal Americans wanted to make their own choices and avoid government oppression. The people of this counter culture had a "do-it-yourself spirit" and did not want society telling them what to do with their families (Gaither 336). Liberal parents "saw formal schools as symbols of everything wrong and destructive in modern life and kept their kids at home" (Gaither 336). This movement paved the way for John Holt, a school critic "who by the mid 1970s had given up on schools entirely and was urging parents to liberate their children from them" (Gaither 336). Holt published the magazine Growing Without Schooling in August of 1977, and it "became the first national homeschooling periodical" (Gaither 336). Not only did John Holt and the liberals of the 1970s contribute to the history of homeschooling, the religious right made an impact as well (Gaither 336).

The religious right consisted of American Protestants (Gaither 336). They wanted to create a new kind of Christian culture "that allowed 'kids to be normal, blue-jean wearing, music-loving American teenagers without abandoning the faith, … to be devout without being nerdy'" (Gaither 336). The philosophy of the American Protestants of the 1970s was certainly different from other Christian groups, and thus the Christian counterculture was born (Gaither 337). According to Gaither, "one important facet of this new Christian counterculture was its political activism," and thus, the Christians became involved in the homeschooling movement (Gaither 337). Some Christians of the 1970s were attracted to homeschooling because they "believed that the Bible gave responsibility for education to parents only" (Gaither 338). Lead by Raymond Moore, the Christians dominated the homeschool scene until the 1990s when Christian schools began to emerge (Gaither 338).

It seems as if homeschooling in today's society is still dominated by the liberals and the religious right (Carsten 162). The number of homeschooling families has increased since the beginning of the movement. In 2002 an estimated 1.725-2.185 million children were homeschooled in the United States, and it is likely that the number has increased since then (Carsten 162). As the homeschooling movement continues to grow, the importance (and opposition of) homeschooling regulation continues to increase.

## The Regulation of American Homeschooling

Currently, homeschooling is legal in all 50 states (Schwartz 45-54). However, each state has the right to regulate home education. The regulation of homeschooling is not without controversy. Some important issues in home school regulation are parental education requirements, curriculum and attendance, and student achievement. These regulations vary from state to state and are often met with opposition from homeschooling parents. The issue of parental education requirements seems to be the most controversial, and therefore, the topic will be discussed first.

There is a debate surrounding the credential requirements of parents who educate their children at home. Some groups think that homeschooling parents should be state certified teachers; the National Education Association (NEA) is one such group (Kunzman 318). According to author Robert Kunzman, "the NEA asserts that homeschoolers should be required to meet all state curricular and testing requirements. But the NEA goes a step further and contends that instruction should be provided only by those with a state teaching license" (Kunzman 318-319). While some agree with groups like the NEA, others disagree on a large scale. As Kunzman asserts, "the responsibilities of a public school teacher and a homeschool teacher, while overlapping in some respects, are markedly different" (Kunzman 319). This seems to be a true statement. Homeschooling parents do not necessarily need to know how to manage a large classroom; they simply need to keep their own children in line. It does seem as if it would be easier for a parent to keep children on the right track throughout the day than a teacher who knows very little, or nothing, about the child's home life.

Holding state certification does not mean that one is more intelligent than another person, or more capable of teaching certain subjects. A parent who holds a Bachelor's Degree in mathematics is probably more qualified to teach algebra than a licensed teacher who specializes in reading or social studies. Kunzman interviewed a mother who stated the following about her ability to educate at home: "I couldn't teach somebody else's twenty-five children to save my life. I'm not a teacher in the sense of being prepared to teach large groups of strangers. But if I didn't think I was the best teacher for my own children, I wouldn't do it. There is nobody who can teach my kids better than I can" (Kunzman 319). Clearly there is a difference between teaching a classroom full of children and teaching one's own children. It is also obvious that parents want to do what they think is best for their children; if a mother thought she needed state licensure to teacher her children, she certainly would seek out the certification. In general, parents do not wish to harm their children's development. Apparently, the government agrees, because "no state currently mandates that homeschool parents have a teaching license" (Kunzman 319). The requirement of parents to have a teaching certificate is not the only issue in this area of regulation.

Some states require a parent to have a high school diploma or GED in order to educate at home (Kunzman 319). This seems reasonable, as basic skills are needed to understand most concepts. In the issue of parental education, too much regulation can be seen as a bad thing; however, not enough regulation is negative as well. Tennessee seems to have a good handle on balanced regulation in this area. According to Schwartz, "Tennessee requires parents to possess a high school diploma or equivalent to teach kindergarten through eighth grades and a bachelor's degree to teach grades nine through twelve" (Schwartz 15). This seems like a good middle ground, because only basic skills are needed to understand and teach most elementary and middle school level concepts. Nevertheless, a high school level curriculum is more difficult and parents may need further study beyond high school to fully understand concepts such as chemistry, calculus, and economics. It only seems logical that a parent should be educated above the level that they are teaching. If a parent is teaching high school, they should have completed at least some college.

There are some legal issues involved in the regulation of parental education as well. According to Schwartz, the problem is two-fold and deals with the issue of the requirement of parents to be state certified teachers (Schwartz 16). It has been argued that the requirement of teacher certification "disqualifies virtually all parents who seek to educate their children in a homeschool setting" (Schwartz 16-17). This argument seems valid, and leaves one to wonder why a parent would need to seek teacher certification to do what parents did for centuries, educate their children without the help of the government. Additionally, Schwartz cites "that a certification requirement for homeschool teachers goes beyond what a state can constitutionally do in assuring that children receive adequate education" (Schwartz 17). This argument also seems valid because requiring something that virtually excludes all parents certainly oversteps the regulation boundaries set by the constitution. Like parental education regulations, the regulation of curriculum and attendance are at the forefront of home education regulation.

According to Schwartz, "many states have attempted to further regulate homeschools by enacting both mandated attendance requirements and establishing base curriculum that must be taught" (Schwartz 13). The regulation of curriculum and attendance are not met without opposition. It seems as if the area of curriculum is the most controversial in home education, because many parents vary in what and how they want to teach their children. Just as the state has the right to regulate the education requirements of parents, the state also has the right to regulate curriculum. Curriculum regulation varies from state to state. According to Kunzman, "current regulations imposed by states involving homeshool curricula range from Indiana's remarkably vague mandate for 'instruction equivalent to that given in public schools' (with no further details and no authority to review curricula) to Pennsylvania's requirements of a portfolio of student work, standardized testing and written report from an outside evaluator" (Kunzman 320). It is through loose regulation of curriculum that homeschooling can have a negative effect on children; however, this issue will be discussed in a later section. According to Schwartz, "thirty-nine states require some type of mandated instruction" (Schwartz 14). However, the state is limited to near minimal regulation. According to Schwartz, "in states that have specific curriculum requirements, the statues only list minimum subjects that must be taught. Any statute or regulation attempting to limit subjects taught in homeschools would certainly be in violation of parents' First Amendment rights" (Schwartz 14-15). Therefore, it appears as if it is the First Amendment that gives parents the freedom to choose what subjects their children learn.

As mentioned previously, the issue of attendance is also open to regulation. According to Schwartz, thirty-six states regulate attendance of homeschoolers (Schwartz 13-14). However, like other areas of regulation, attendance requirements vary from state to state. For example, Georgia requires students to receive instruction at least 4.5 hours per day, 180 days per year (Schwartz 14). Whereas in Maryland, the state requires that students receive instruction for only "a "sufficient" amount of time to implement the instructional program" (Schwartz 14). As one can see, regulation regarding attendance is quite vague. In addition to curriculum and attendance regulation, the regulation of testing is important to homeschoolers.

Testing is often used to measure the progress of school aged children, including homeschoolers. Schwartz states that "thirty states have statutes or regulations that attempt to measure the academic progress of homeschool students" (Schwartz 19). One cannot fault states for inquiring about the academic progress of students; it is the responsibility of the state to make sure that children receive adequate education. Yet, according to Kunzman, "current approaches to testing homeschoolers are generally ineffective and misguided as well" (Kunzman 322). This seems like a valid claim, because it is difficult to evaluate students using tests in general. Consequently, it would be even more difficult to assess students who learn in non-traditional ways using traditional methods to measure achievement. One such traditional method of assessment is standardized tests; this method is one of the most popular (Schwartz 19).

According to Kunzman, most states do not stipulate the particular test or testing conditions—as a result, parents often choose and administer a test themselves" (Kunzman 323). This seems like an invalid method of assessing a students' progress. In public schools, students are tested under controlled conditions; tests are often timed and can go on for hours or days. It would be very easy for a homeschooling parent to give their child extra time for test questions, allow them to take the test for shorter periods of time, or simply help their child answer questions. Other methods of assessment, such as portfolio review of progress and annual re-application to homeschool seem more valid than standardized testing (Kunzman 323).

The nature of homeschooling is to allow parents to teach their children using unconventional methods, and in turn, homeschool students learn in unconventional ways. It seems only logical that unconventional assessment tools would measure the educational progress of homeschoolers better than conventional methods. A child who learns through mostly hands-on activities might have trouble sitting down to a standardized test. A portfolio review would probably be a better indicator of progress for a hands-on student, because materials can be collected over time. There is not one right way to teach a child and therefore, there may not be one right way to assess achievement.

## Why Educate at Home?

Just as state homeschooling regulations of the current era vary from state to state, the reasons for homeschooling vary from family to family. The reasons are many. Author Ed Collom identifies two types of modern homeschooling families, the pedagogues and the ideologues (Collom 309). The pedagogues in general are similar to the homeschooling parents of the counterculture of the 1960s and 1970s (Collom 309). These parents are against "the bureaucratization and professionalization of public schools" (Collom 309). Additionally, it seems viable that the pedagogues of today might choose to homeschool in opposition of the No Child Left Behind Act of 2001 (Boers 108). According to author David Boers, the act "mandated standardized tests and state standards to regulate the curriculum in order to produce high test scores" (Boers 109). Basically, the No Child Left Behind Act teaches students to take tests in an attempt to measure the achievement of American public schools (Boers 109). Critics of the No Child Left Behind Act argue that "standards and standardized tests without regard to cultural framework of minority populations align themselves with the history of deculturalization and assimilation as has been evident in the evolution of American education" (Boers 109). The No Child Left Behind Act essentially creates a disadvantage for low income and minority students, while ignoring the educational process in favor of high test scores (Boers 109). The pedagogues do not always agree with the government; it is certainly viable that such a group would not be in favor of standardized test based education (Collom 309). Unlike the pedagogues, the ideologues prefer to homeschool for religious reasons (Collom 309). According to Collom, ideologues have a desire to "crusade against the secular forces of modern society, seeking to impart religious values on their children" (Collom 309). They are not unlike the American Protestants of the 1970s. Although the ideologues and pedagogues homeschool for different reasons initially, there are many reasons to homeschool that cross idealistic lines.

Collom surveyed multiple research sources to determine reasons why parents choose to educate their children at home. Some common reasons for homeschooling include "fear of negative peer influences," dissatisfaction with the public school system and accommodation of special education needs (gifted and disabled children) (Collom 310-311). Not all parents with these concerns had a religious background; however, parents citing "fear of negative peer influences" did describe themselves as religious. The reasons cited in the research that Collom examined are not very different for the reasons that parents started homeschooling in the 1960s and 1970s. In general it seems as if parents choose to homeschool their children because they care about their well-being and education. This is not to say that parents who choose other modes of education love their children less; some parents have more patience and resources than others. According to author Brian D. Ray, "all parents, including homeschoolers, want their children to be competent in reading, writing, and mathematics and to comprehend the fundamental principles of science, history, art, and geography. Homeschoolers also want to retain the responsibility of raising their children and not have their children raised by strangers" (Ray 50). Sometimes parents just want to take on all the roles of parenting, including education. It could be said that parents educate at home because they are trying to shelter their children from the world. Perhaps this is true in some respects. However, parents in general are not out to harm their children. They want to do what they think is best.

**Advantages of Homeschooling**
There are many advantages to homeschooling, otherwise parents would not be interested in the practice. One of the main advantages of homeschooling is the opportunity to customize the education of one's child. According to Ray, "homeschooling is an interactive process rather than a series of tasks to be tackled up" (Ray 52). Homeschooling parents have the opportunity to choose what and when their children learn. Additionally, home educated

children have a say in their education as well. Homeschooling is "intensely personal, closely supervised, intentional, delight-directed, and not based on a one-size-fits-all model," therefore no two homeschools are exactly alike (Ray 52). Not all children learn in the same way. Some children are visual learners; others are good at listening or hands-on activities. Homeschooling gives parents the opportunity and freedom to allow their children to learn in a way that is best for them, unlike public or private schools, which teach children based on educational philosophies laid out by the school or school district. Customization also allows parents to meet the needs of gifted children and children with special needs (Ray 52). These children could otherwise be lost in public and private schools, which must accommodate all students rather than focus on individuals. In addition to customization, there are other benefits to homeschooling.

Another advantage of homeschooling is that parents have the opportunity to combine their role as a parent with the role of a teacher ("Homeschool Pros and Cons"). Many parents think that their parenting skills provide an excellent foundation for teaching their own children ("Homeschool Pros and Cons"). This seems likely, because parents know how to control and communicate with their children on an intimate level. It is easy to see why this type of a close relationship would benefit a child's learning experience. Additionally, homeschooling is beneficial because it allows children to be more involved in their communities. Since parents have the freedom to teach what and when they want, children have more time to take on leadership roles and do volunteer work (Dumas 81). According to Dumas, "a nationwide study of homeschooled adults found that—across every measure—these adults were more likely to be involved in civic activities than same aged adults in the population" (Dumas 81). Home educated children simply have more time for non-academic activities. However, these non-academic activities have the power to enhance a child's education and prepare them for future employment (Dumas 81).

One of the most important advantages of homeschooling is that the practice has the ability to breakdown racial and socioeconomic barriers (Collom 331). According to Collom, "minority students and those from low-income families have consistently been found to be at a disadvantage in the public education system. Homeschooling apparently levels the playing field, ameliorating the negative effects that race and class subordination have shown in the public schools" (Collom 331-332). Essentially, home-schooling provides minority and low income students with an educational advantage, whereas public schools fuel the disadvantage (Collom 331). One can speculate that this advantage is the result of the amount of individual attention that homeschoolers receive. It seems as if the public school system often overlooks bright students (or simply does not have the time to acknowledge them); minority and low income children are intelligent. Public schools sometimes fail to see this; however, minority and low income children that are homeschooled have the opportunity to shine.

### Disadvantages of Homeschooling

Just as there are advantages to home education, there are also disadvantages. One disadvantage of homeschooling is that it is an enormous time commitment for parents. The time that parents must put into homeschooling can result in difficult parent-child relationships ("Homeschool Pros and Cons"). Not all parents are well suited to be homeschoolers; some parents need more social interaction than they get while educating at home ("Homeschool Pros and Cons"). There are parents who are cut out for the life of a worker and need the adult interaction—not everyone can spend their days with a child ("Homeschool Pros and Cons").

While the ability to customize a child's education to accommodate talents and disabilities is an advantage, it can also be viewed as a disadvantage. State certified teachers have the professional skills to teach such children; parents may not always possess such skills ("Homeschool Pros and Cons"). Additionally, parents may not have attained the necessary level of education to teach children with unique educational needs. A parent who did not finish high school is probably not equipped to teach a teenager advanced calculus. Public schools often have resources such as counselors, special education teachers and aides, and gifted and talented programs that parents merely do not have access to. In situations with special learning needs, it might be better for parents to place some trust on professional educators ("Homeschool Pros and Cons").

Additionally, socialization can be a disadvantage for homeschoolers ("Homeschool Pros and Cons"). According to Ray, "studies have revealed that in terms of social, emotional, and psychological well-being, home-schooled students are doing well" (Ray 50). However, it cannot be denied that homeschoolers do not always have the opportunity to interact with children their own age ("Homeschool Pros and Cons"). This might make home educated children seem awkward around their peers. Furthermore, home educated students do not always have access to group activities such as sports, theater, and band ("Homeschool Pros and Cons"). It seems as if many homeschoolers can overcome this barrier by participating in community activities. Some parents also seek the services of the local public school to supplement the educational and social needs of their children (Schwartz 23). Although socialization can be a disadvantage, it seems as if parents can help their children overcome this by putting in the effort to seek out alternative resources and experiences.

Another disadvantage of homeschooling is the fact that regulations vary and the state does not always know what takes place in a homeschool; this leaves room for child neglect and educational neglect (Carsten 178). The homeschool environment gives neglectful parents the opportunity to hide abuse from authorities. Other parents might simply neglect to teach their children anything, which is considered educational neglect (Carsten 179). According to author Major Michael D. Carsten, "educational neglect is an identified form of child neglect" (Carsten 178). Most parents do have good intentions, but one should keep in mind neglect when deciding to homeschool their children. A parent may intend to teach their children, but fail to do so in the process. Parents who think they are committed to homeschooling should be careful not to accidentally (or intentionally) neglect their child's education.

## Conclusion

In conclusion, homeschooling is a very unique practice. However, the decision to homeschool should not be taken lightly. It is a commitment, with many advantages and disadvantages. Parents have been educating their children from the beginning of time; however, homeschooling may not be the best option for everyone. Parents need to keep in mind state laws and regulations when homeschooling their children; it is also important to consider the educational needs of one's child and whether the parent educated enough to meet those needs. Additionally, not all parents are cut out to be home educators. The most important thing a parent can do is to make an educated decision regarding the upbringing, socialization, and education of one's children. Personal feelings about the education system, religion, and the government should not outweigh the well-being of the child. A child-centered decision is required when choosing to educate at home, not an ideological one.

## Works Cited

Boers, David. *History of American Education Primer*. New York: Peter Lang, 2007. Print.

Carsten, Major Michael D. "An Education in Home Schooling." *Military Law Review* 177 (Fall 2003): 162-183. Web. 28 Feb. 2011.

Collom, Ed. "The Ins and Outs of Homeschooling: The Determinants of Parental Motivations and Student Achievement." *Education and Urban Society* 37.3 (2005): 307-335. Web. 4 April 2011.

Cooper, Bruce S. and John Sureau. "The Politics of Homeschooling: New Developments, New Challenges." *Educational Policy* 21.110 (2007): 110-131. Web. 24 Feb. 2011.

Dumas, Tanya K., Sean Gates, and Deborah R. Schwarzer. "Evidence for Homeschooling: Constitutional Analysis in Light of Social Science Research." *Widener Law Review* 16.1 (2010): 63-87. Web. 28 Feb. 2011.

Kunzman, Robert. "Understanding homeschooling: A better approach to regulation." *Theory and Research in Education* 7.331 (2009): 311-330. Web. 24 Feb. 2011.

Gaither, Milton. "Homeschooling in the USA: Past, present, and future." *Theory and Research in Education* 7.331 (2009): 331-346. Web. 24 Feb. 2011.

"Homeschool Pros and Cons." *www.letshomeschool.com*. Let's Homeschool, 2009. Web. 4 April 2011.

Ray, Brian D. "Customization Through Homeschooling." *Educational Leadership* (April 2002): 50-54. Web. 24 Feb. 2011.

Schwartz, Brian D. *The Law of Homeschooling*. Dayton: Education Law Association, 2008. Print.

Spring, Joel. *The American School From the Puritans to No Child Left Behind*. 7th ed. Boston: McGraw-Hill Higher Education, 2008. Print.

Ian McNabb
HNR 225

The European Singularity

Following the inception of Einstein's general theory of relativity in 1915, theoretical physicists of the early twentieth century discovered the possibility of gravitational singularities. These anomalies, commonly called "black holes," result from extremely dense masses deforming local space-time. The nearly infinite magnitude of gravitational force creates a funnel shape in space time and pulls nearby objects in to a chaotic "pit,"where known physical laws become meaningless. Sometimes the attributes of these "black holes" become metaphors for other indefinable rates of change, most notably the "technological singularity." This term, coined by Vernor Vinge (1), refers to the moment when artificial intelligence exceeds human intelligence, and the future of such a "virtual" world becomes incomprehensible to humanity. However this concept of an astronomical leap in a civilization does not belong exclusively to the invention of artificial intelligence, but also can apply to several moments in human history. Zweig's Europe, the "Golden Age of Security" (2), was approaching one of these human singularities. The World of Yesterday provides an account of a prosperous world whose obsession with certainty and worship of Progress bloated it to the point of self-collapse.

Most physical singularities that have been observed by modern science are created during the collapse of super-massive stars--the result of a large mass compressed into a tiny space, a condition similar to the state of Europe on the eve of war. If the Great War was the singularity that radically changed the nature of Europe, then there must have been some buildup of political or social "mass" to justify such a violent disruption of "European space-time." The industrial growth and arms race between the Powers can stand for a literal "build-up," and the "mass" simply the runway European war machine. Zweig rarely mentions this re-armament; he remarks only in passing on arms manufacturers Krupp and Schneider-Creusot rehearsing their cannons (3). However as he gets closer to the war, the author begins to take notice of another kind of buildup: public opinion. When he visits the cinema in Tours (4), he sees the effect of propaganda on the once docile and uninterested people of France, who become hysterical at a short shot of Kaiser Wilhelm on a newsreel. Zweig is troubled by this reaction and laments that his generation had become subject to "mass emotion and hysteria" (5) but never individually let their thoughts flirt with the prospect of war. Perhaps it was not merely political tensions and war machines, but the public's easily swayed perception of politics that pushed Europe to critical mass. Despite what the true source of this "mass" may have been, it was rapidly approaching singularity.

Every large mass distorts space-time in some way, such as the sun pulling the planets into orbit. Just as a star affects the motion of planets, the European "mass" affected the political and social motion of Zweig's youth. The author adamantly believes that the religion of his time was Progress, that "every advance became more marked, more rapid, more varied" (6). He describes the Vienna of yesterday as a "cosmopolitan city," where European cultures melted together in the minds of musicians and poets. Because they perceived nothing but acceleration in social progress, his generation almost wallowed in optimism. However acceleration cannot exist without constant force, in this case the European "mass." As Zweig's world became more technologically and socially sophisticated, the mass increased and thus caused its own social forces to increase in turn, and therefore created faster and faster change. Europeans endlessly strove to improve their own society; as a result they accentuated this inward cultural acceleration.

Since the gravitational force of a black hole is so great, even rays of light cannot escape it at certain distances. This property makes them nearly impossible to detect with the eye, not unlike Zweig's generation that did not expect war, even if it did appear just beyond their view. The threshold beyond which light is trapped is known as the event horizon, the "point of no return." Much like a wandering spacecraft ignorant of a physical singularity, Zweig's remained ignorant of its own European singularity until it was too late. He writes that the Viennese concerned themselves more with art and cultural matters than current events, and that no one really thought of war or death because they were too busy enjoying life. His schools taught him nothing but strict and meaningless routines, and people often hid most of their bodies under layers of clothing. They had forced themselves into an aesthetic mentality and chose only to recognize things that contributed to progress. By doing so they became what Dostoevsky feared in Winter Notes on Summer Impressions (7); they blindly followed the promises of

Progress like a herd of cattle. Zweig remarks that as each nation approached their vision of perfection, a "storm of pride and confidence rushed over Europe, followed by clouds; perhaps the rise had come to quickly" (8). Europe was becoming overwhelmed by "surplus of force" and "internal dynamism" (9) as each nation became hopeless obsessed with becoming more perfect than their neighbor. Progress became German Progress and British Progress and French Progress and so on. People accepted their own nation's flavor because they only knew how to follow Progress. They blindly marched through the event horizon, and Progress collapsed like physics in a black hole.

If 1914 truly was Europe's event horizon, then not a single beam of light from the glorious World of Security would have survived. Zweig himself says that "the great storm has long since smashed it" (10). Nothing remained immune to the singularity's effect; it created a fundamental shift in the European ideology. The laws of the old world were lost as a single gunshot sent an entire civilization into a suicidal orgy. Inside a black hole, matter is freed from Newton's laws and becomes independent of gravity, magnetism, even time. In the European singularity, people were stripped of the laws that sustained the Golden Age: security, certainty, and positive Progress. Matter becomes chaos without the physical laws, and Europe became chaotic without its old laws. People saw the true fruits of Progress, as iron beasts became the new cavalry and even the air became a weapon with the use of mustard gas. Matter does not behave in a singularity, and neither do people. Millions of young men, who like Zweig tried to hang on to the old laws, were killed as the value of a human life was reduced to the price of a bullet.

Vinge postulated that the technological singularity would abolish our current understanding of the universe, just like the European singularity abolished the World of Security. Unlike a physical singularity, however, a human singularity such as World War I does not end in eternal chaos and destruction. While the people of Europe did abandon the old laws, they also had to create new laws to sustain the World of Insecurity. Security and serenity became violence and catastrophe as Europeans accepted war and suffering as inevitable. Zweig conceded that the old optimistic world was no longer sustainable under the new laws. He knew that such striving for perfection would only lead to self destruction, and the best he could do was to try to capture that great atmosphere when Europe was at its peak. Unfortunately for Zweig, the next singularity would come too soon.

## Notes

1. Vernor Vinge. "The Coming Technological Singularity: How to Survive in the Post-Human Era." San Diego State University. http://www-rohan.sdsu.edu/faculty/vinge/misc/singularity.html.
2. Stefan Zweig. The World of Yesterday. (Lincoln, Nebr.: University of Nebraska Press, 1964), p. 1.
3. Zweig, Yesterday, p. 205.
4. Zweig, Yesterday, p. 210.
5. Zweig, Yesterday, p. 211.
6. Zweig, Yesterday, p. 3.
7. Dostoevsky, Fyodor. Winter Notes on Summer Impressions. (New York: McGraw Hill, 1965), p. 90.
8. Zweig, Yesterday, p. 196.
9. Zweig, Yesterday, p. 197.
10. Zweig, Yesterday, p. 5.

## Bibliography

Dostoevsky, Fyodor. *Winter Notes on Summer Impressions*. New York: McGraw Hill, 1965.

Vinge, Vernor. "The Coming Technological Singularity: How to Survive in the Post-Human Era." San Diego State University. http://www-rohan.sdsu.edu/faculty/vinge/misc/singularity.html.

Zweig, Stefan. *The World of Yesterday.* Lincoln, Nebr.: University of Nebraska Press, 1964.

Josh Lycka
HNR 311

Women Write the Gulag and the Siege of Leningrad

My earliest memory is from 1917. Mother tucks a daisy in my tousled hair and I feel her hands pass along the crown of my head; she hums with her voice as she accompanies the phonograph. Time passes subtly; all at once I am running across our small street to the prize that awaits me: the embrace of my Grandfather. But panic, hate, and confusion suddenly strike me. A stranger grabs me, lifts me into the air, and my eyes fill with tears. In this life I can only recall ever being captured twice: as 4 year old Naddie, just before a car would have struck me outside of my childhood home in Samara, and as 21 year old Nadia, cleaning the dishes in the peace of that same home on a Sunday afternoon.

If the neighbor would not have moved me from harm's way, a car would have struck me and changed my family's life forever. I wept, the daisy tumbling onto the pavement, now forgotten. Who is this? I want Grandpapa! I screamed inside my head as I cried. Father ran from the house and the various adult voices blurred into noise. I still wanted Grandpapa. My memory plays like a film: Mother carries me inside, both of our eyes stained red with tears. My father spanks me and I cannot understand what I did wrong, why a stranger ruined my plans, and especially why my father is now inflicting pain on me. Between sobs I utter, "Grandpapa! Oh Papa, oh papa," but my words are incomprehensible, overpowered by my tantrum.

Years of meditation have allowed me to delve ever deeper into my memories and explore my past; reminiscence allows me to acknowledge the peace of the present, for throughout my life I have survived horrors, pitfalls, and hell upon earth. I derive my perception of beauty from the contrast.

My life in the Gulag diverged from every comfort and custom I had experienced so far in my life. I was daydreaming about far-off romances at my parents' home on the day of my arrest. The cuckoo clock struck a single note and echoed through the hallway. I turned off the faucet and heard the fading noise for only an instant- for a knock at the door followed immediately behind. I imagined a mysterious lover coming to carry me off to the mountains, or perhaps a package that arrived from a far-off land. I opened the door theatrically and began to curtsy, then froze. The cold black attire of the officers shook me from my daydream and stifled the air around me. An officer announced, "We need to enter your house," as if he expected me to hold the door open for him and invite him inside.

I still close my eyes and see the face of the arresting officer. I study the three men, standing firmly in resolve with pistols and handcuffs as one smokes the stump of a five cent cigar. "Miss Kuzsova, you have been uncovered as an enemy of the State and are under arrest for terrorism and acts of treason against the Soviet." Imagining what I possibly could have done, I retrace the steps of my previous day, then the last week, the last month, the last year, I walk slowly to the kitchen and see the half washed basin of dishes, the linoleum tile, the curtains; everything blurs together into a blotch of color. Only the hand of the officer pulls me from the kitchen and pushes me up the stairs to my brother's room. "Pack a small bag with underwear and a jacket and come downstairs. If you have foreign currency or unclaimed jewelry, bring it now and you can help yourself out," called a voice from downstairs. The door of my father's study creaks and I hear the clink of his cognac set as they hastily open and pour it. The officers are looting the house.

A set of small golden butterfly earrings catch my eye from my mother's bed stand and I hold the fragile pieces of metal in my hand. I bend the wings together and slide them between the wire and fabric of my brassiere, and grab the pin and needle from her drawer to sew up the hole. The voices become louder from downstairs and I hear them rummage through the liquor cabinet. Rather than guard an enemy of the state, they help themselves to a drink. Their façade hardly convinces me for a second.

I collect my belongings and take great care to sneak as many necessities as possible into the lining of my bag and into my hair. An officer startles me at the door of my room and announces that we must leave. As in a dream, I float in front of him down the stairs and to the door. The four of us emerge onto the empty street; my grandparents' house lies across the street and reminds me of my capture as a girl, the first time a stranger had separated me from my desires.

Why couldn't a more pleasant memory have stuck in my mind- why don't I remember my first steps with Papa instead of my first spanking? I do remember once when I found a bright red ribbon on the ground at the market and pinned it on my dress, greedy to show my father when I arrived home. To me, it was a gift from the gods: a symbol of my self-sufficiency and fiery attitude. I had no idea that it actually represented the revolution and knew even less that its pigment reflected death, imprisonment, and loss.

He would not see this ribbon until 1928, the year he was released from his first 10 year term in prison. I returned home with my mother all those years ago to find 2 black government vehicles stationed at our home. "Naddie, hold my hand," my mother whispered, her voice tenuously balancing fear and courage. "Papa is a good man, Naddie, please remember this above everything. These men are animals that use violence…lies….they are different…"

I fingered my ribbon, polished it between my thumb and forefinger and ignored her. He'll love my ribbon, he'll swing me around and it will stay pinned on and look like a rosignol flying over the trees…

He emerged from our front door in the hands of the police officers. He violently jerked his arms in an attempt to escape. "Nadia! Yuliya!" He cried out as he tore his flesh against the handcuffs. "Papa! Papa! Look!" I wailed naïvely and watched the situation unfold in front of me. I was not helpless because I was a child, but because we were all helpless in that time against our government, The Soviet Union.

By the age of 21 I had already seen the destructive potential of the NKVD and of Stalin's democide. Through my school years my peers stigmatized me as common criminal's daughter and I suspect that my teachers shared an uncertainty about me. My mother continually reminded me in private that it was a fabrication, but her words meant little compared to those of my peers and teachers. I wanted to believe her but held trust in the elegant design of the Soviet state and sympathized with their precaution in an epoch of treason and espionage. When my friends' parents began to disappear, followed by professors, merchants, and family friends, my sympathy diminished. I understood before many that the NKVD held the ticket to our freedom: an asset that they might redeem for hard labor, torture, or imprisonment at their slightest whim. After nearly a decade of my paranoia and fear, the state finally revoked my liberty in an unexpected coup de grace.

I was brought to the entrance of the prison and searched hastily, the contents of my satchel emptied onto a table. My scalp tingled when a woman officer started to search my hair with a fine toothed comb. I had foolishly underestimated the rigor of the NKVD. The comb caught on a set of pins positioned deep within the folds of my hair. She tugged and pulled out a tress along with the contraband.

My pulse heightened and beat against the golden earrings that seemed obvious to me now within the tuck of my shirt. The officer felt my body for weapons, books, especially papers, but did not intend to undress me. My body fought to stand still against the brute; I nearly darted toward a door or reached to strike her, but I subdued the impulse. The search had ended.

She led me down a tile hallway lined with portraits and room numbers. I finally entered an office and she signed to her superior, turned, and left us alone. The man's aura initially seemed calm and stern; he nodded and stood up respectfully to shake my hand. "Would you like a glass of water?" He gestured toward a pitcher filled with ice water. "I would like a cigarette," I started, "and a glass of water." "Lemon?" He spoke with irony, but moved toward a tray and reached for one. I detested his pretenses- I willed at that moment to push against their oppression until I had no strength to do so, in spite of their attitude.

"I know that this arrest has been sudden, and I apologize for the shock it must have caused. But don't worry; your family has been notified. I see here that your father was once imprisoned himself after the revolution. Where was he held?"

I looked through his face and saw the beast that he represented, the potential of his cruelty.

"This file also indicates that you studied music at the Kazan Academy of Art and Culture. I had an old friend who taught music there, Professor Beaubien. Perhaps you had a class with him?"

I closed my eyes. I see Beaubien in front of a piano, his nasally accent shrieking over the chords. My past ends at the door of this office, I thought. I alone know what memories remain with me. I had to respond to his question after my audacious request, and replied, "No, I didn't have the chance to study with him while at university. Were you a student there?" I tasted acid in my throat.

"Unfortunately," he snapped, "we don't have the occasion to discuss this and that over cocktails at the moment. Your courtesy is appreciated but unnecessary. For a girl that forgets sets of pins and a clip in her hair you seem to act startled by my question."

He had tempted me with his false sincerity and I fell for it. The beast had dropped the act and now aimed to orient me to my new life as a prisoner as brusquely as possible. "Your spirit of treason follows you," he continued, "even in the halls of justice, and even in this office you flaunt it." "What treason?" I moved the hair from my eyes, straightened, and uttered the question with a meek ferocity.

"You mock me with obvious questions, you lie to me, and you undermine my trust of the soviet people!" He snarled and pushed back his chair slightly. "You have shed your decency and alas we shall rehabilitate you to regain it. I'll recommend you to my superior for the next meeting." The door opened on the cue of his last word and another officer appeared with a smile on his face. My throat again burned from the rising acid, and I reached for the glass of water. I drank it all in one movement and leaned forward with my cigarette for a light. "Perhaps towards another cause, in another time, in another country, your egoism would be appreciated," he signed to the officer and reached forward with a match. "I trust we will meet quite soon," he stated blankly, as if he had receded back into solemnity for the next client. I puffed and studied his desk for an instant until the new officer placed his hand on my shoulder and led me out of the office.

I was placed into a solitary confinement cell off of a hallway on the main level of the prison. The back wall of my room followed the curvature of the building and resembled the shape of a hastily cut pie. The bed was bolted on the floor to make the worst use of space; it was jammed against the curve of the wall and the corner so I had only enough space to either lie down on the floor or the bed. The room was wholly visible from a peephole in the door. I sat on the bed and stared at the door without blinking; and as I breathed deeply, it formed new shapes and blurred into colors. My body ached from holding tense for so many hours in the car, search, and prison offices.

Within the first week of confinement I learned the basic routine and habits of the guards: reveilles, bread, slop out, toilet, walk to the courtyard, confinement, monitoring; they peeped through the hole at 30 minute intervals, but I heard guards pacing, smoking, and reading almost constantly. A cough triggered a peephole to open, an eye to appear, and slam shut. If I rustled my bed sheets I could procure the mysterious eye for even longer as it hungrily searched the room for something out of place: a reason for the punishment cell.

The superior officer saw me in his office during the second week in prison. I pushed through the heavy mahogany door into an expansive room draped with flags and tapestries. "Nadia Kuzsova, arrested for terrorism and treason. I received a report from an arresting officer last week that indicated a lack of respect, inability to follow procedure, and general disdain for authority." I looked at my feet. "Luckily you have been brought to the proper institution for rehabilitation, Ms. Kuzsova. If your current confinement cell won't suit you, we have arranged special accommodations for more… dramatic cases." The officer smirked and plucked a loosely rolled cigarette from his ear. The tobacco fluttered onto the report on his desk; the embers grazed the sheet after he lit it and they tumbled, glowing, onto the paper. I watched the firestorm and remained silent. He started again in a more casual tone. "I would offer you one if I didn't have the sense that you would deny it. You trust that I didn't lace it with arsenic?" My audacity stirred deep within me but I held my tongue and shifted my gaze to his chin. He recognized my desire and pulled a pack of Lucky Strikes from his breast pocket as he flicked the ashes of his own cigarette upon my report.

"To end all of this we need a signed confession from you. While at university you staged protests and engaged in acts of terrorism with a certain professor whom we apprehended earlier this year." He produced a carbon copy of a blurry document and I immediately recognized the handwriting of my professor at the bottom. "A signed confession from the organizer holds firmly in court."

He had once taught me to move my hands over the ivory keys so gently, poised to strike in time with the sheet music. Now Beaubien damned those fingers to hard labor and molestation in the rugged heart of the Gulag. A tear crept to my eye and I instinctively reached for the cigarettes on the edge of the table. When his fist struck my wrist I heard the crack, the thud, and my shriek; I observed from the recesses of my mind where I was still safe.

The blood rushed to my wrist and inflated the skin like a black balloon. I moved it slightly to find that it had not been shattered, just cracked or fissured; with no evident medical attention in the prison, I could have been forever disabled. My sobs burst out involuntarily- I would have stifled them if I had had the power. "Treachery!" He roared, working himself into a rage. He walked over to my side of the table and grabbed my forearms, his embers burning my arm and my blouse. "Cigarettes? Signature!" I made my body fall limp against his hands and the chair. His grip tightened and pulled me toward him and my head sank back.

The paper was worthless. I figured that if I signed then everything would move in my favor, for I had already damned myself enough. "I…" my throat dried just as I had wanted to speak; I struggled to pull the words from my depths. "I'll sign." He unscrupulously struck me again and knocked me into the chair. I cursed loudly, found my strength, and repeated, "I'll sign!"

He didn't care about a confession anymore because he was drunk on rage and power. I gazed into his eyes, bloodshot and wicked. "I'll sign!" my voice had become hoarse at the last word; I forced it with just the kind of power that I reviled and started to vomit weakly onto myself, tucked into the chair.

"You treasonous whore, I'll beat it out of you for your own sake!" Now the tears flowed voluntarily. With each strike, with each verbal blow, he threatened my humanity. That devil would never take it from me. He stepped away from me, for he now risked a messy uniform: I was nearly covered in blood, tears and vomit. My hand shook but I picked up the pen from the desk and signed boldly: Nadia Kuzsova.

I learned to communicate in the prison by gently tapping on the cell walls in a coded alphabet. I had neighbors on both sides of my cell, but only one was proficient at the language. I closed my eyes to imagine a grid of dots and letters that I would tap out to form words, sentences, and reflections. A man named Fedorov was imprisoned beside me. He had entered the prison only a week earlier than I and had quickly adjusted to our new language. I learned only a little about his life, for our conversations were punctuated by frequent inspections from the guards. One day I sat tapping, eyes closed, attached to the faint sound, when the peephole snapped open and the guard's eye appeared. "There is no sitting on the floor, n or tapping, n or sleeping during the day!" he roared. I rose and took the blow of the door to my shoulder as he rushed in to apprehend me. I cried, screamed, kicked. But my mind stayed calm and repeated the sentence I had just tapped: "I would walk along the Volga in the mornings…"

* * *

I glance at my timepiece- 3am. I just returned from a dance in the city and lost track of time along the way. I pull in the courtyard as I imagine my parents' reaction, for I broke my curfew by 3 hours without contacting them. So much time has passed that I can afford a minute in the car to breathe, prepare an alibi and wait for a lecture or punishment. I focus on the mechanical sound of the door lock, handle, and hinge as they break the still night's silence. As I enter the house Papa stands at the sink and gazes out the window, waiting and listening. I see from the reflection that his eyes are closed and his face carries both worry and fatigue.

"Papa…"

He turns and smiles. A tear appears in his eye. "Naddie, I'm so glad you're back."

After he lost me for ten years, he didn't mind waiting three hours into the night to see me. "I had a friend in the labor camp that missed curfew one night after logging in the forest. Guards set off with dogs to find him and I sensed that he was injured or had run," I see my father ten years younger, waiting for his comrade in the hut. He continues, "He got lost and found his way back separate from the guards." I can't bear the reality of his words. I won't probe deeper into the story, I won't find out what happened to him. "Papa, I-"

"Naddie," His hand rests on my shoulder. "I just don't want to lose you again. I'm not the soviet."

Papa's words remained in my memory for all these years as an important distinction between parental motives and the NKDV's. Many of my friends believed wholeheartedly in the euphemisms that the Soviet pitched to justify their rule. They treated the government like a guardian. "He was a traitor," one would say about a friend who had been taken away in the night. For them the act of the arrest justified the punishment, the stigma, and the ruthless actions forced upon a person. I buried my feelings to all of my closest friends but two, whom I knew I could trust to the death. To entrust such treacherous accusations to someone was essentially a wager of one's life.

I was 17 years old when I discovered the profound change my father had made. From that point on I was aligned with him and my mother in our cautious fear; my brother and sister were indoctrinated from an early age at school to believe in the grace of Stalin and the divinity of the Soviets. They were torn between our words and those of their teachers, classmates and friends. I questioned how a moral human could subject young children to such political extremism. But even as true believers in the system I knew that they would never compromise family for political doctrine, and I hoped that they would eventually become politically apathetic and apply their passions to other avenues.

As I did with my memories, I would often recreate scenes from the future in my mind's eye while alone in the cell. I imagined my siblings engaged in a revolution in France, or as immigrants in a sunny Arab state filled with ranches, colorful fields, and freedom. My sole happiness came from these meditations that empowered me with rich imagery, vivid memories, and endless fantasies. The guards allowed me to practice meditation, and some even allowed me to close my eyes, positioned on the bed in a lotus position, my body humming with my repressed breath.

These quiet moments violently contrast with the next 12 years of my life. I left Samara to be transferred to a series of labor camps in the south, which were better than the Siberian camps carved out of tundra in the north. My entrance into prison society was gentle and welcoming. The other women held me in high regard because I helped them settle their minds and taught them new ways to breathe. We sat together at night and hummed, eyes closed, to make a chorus reminiscent of the cicada's song along the river. The daytime brought pain and dehumanization.

During the dehumanizing times I was able to derive an even greater sense of worth for myself. If I hurt in the present, the future must be filled with relief. I never contemplated suicide and never complained, though I wept often. I alone knew that I did not weep out of self-pity but of pity for the others; out of fear for my family, the souls of the guards, the officers, and the political radicals.

\*\*\*

I push open the door and sneak up behind my grandfather. The room smells of sweetgrass and lavender, and a candle smolders the wax around its wick, the smoke snaking toward the ceiling. His deep breath shakes his body; the vibration carries equally into the floor and the air around him. He knows that I am in the room, but stays positioned on the floor with his legs stacked onto his hips. Grandfather learned to breathe this way, he once said, from sherpas he met while travelling in the east. He would later tell me that one could control the world around him with a strong focused breath and a still mind. At this moment, I have only been alive for 5 years and am hardly yet aware of the evils of the world. I throw my arms around his neck and feel the power of his lungs that shake both of our bodies. I have reached my goal, finally.

*Nadia Kuzsova served 14 years in the Gulag. She served 2 years in solitary confinement, followed by 12 years of hard labor. When she was finally released from her sentence she was exiled, and lived the rest of her life in China along the Yellow River.*

# Department of Writing

The Department of Writing offers instruction in academic, creative, and professional writing. Academic writing courses, which are designed for all students in the university community, include first-year composition and junior-level writing. For students who choose to major in writing, the department offers emphasis areas in creative and professional writing. The department also offers a minor in writing for students wishing to enhance their writing abilities for personal or professional reasons.

Academic writing, creative writing, and professional writing all belong to the liberal arts. As disciplines, they seek to sensitize student writers to the values and practices of particular genres of writing. The overall goal is to develop in students the ability to write well in a variety of contexts. Students develop this ability by reading and analyzing models and by drafting and revising original work in a workshop setting. Academic writing explores the art of writing well in specific disciplinary contexts. Creative writing explores the art of writing literary fiction, poetry, drama, and non-fiction. Professional writing explores the art of writing nonfiction and workplace writing.

The department has 45 faculty and approximately 210 majors. Altogether we offer about 250 sections a year in academic, creative, and professional writing.

Dan Royer, Chair
Professor of Writing

Lake Ontario Hall 326
Department of Writing
Grand Valley State University
1 Campus Drive
Allendale, MI 49401-9403
616-331-3411
www.gvsu.edu/writing